Windhill Farms

Written and illustrated by:
Phyllis M. Ellis

Copyright © Phyllis M. Ellis

Book design by Phyllis M. Ellis

Illustration on the cover by E.C. Van Swearingen

Pen and ink drawings by Phyllis M. Ellis

Published May 2016

www.phyllisellisartsandbooks.com

Printed by CreateSpace, An Amazon.com Company

Windhill Farms

By Phyllis M. Ellis

Introduction

The author, Phyllis, happened to come across her dad's journals and realized on that particular day of April 2nd, he would have been 111 years old. She felt that he was saying to her, "Please do something with my journals." Phyllis' journey began as she spent months rewriting her dad's journals with dialog to bring the characters in the story to life. Memories would flood around in her head each night as though her dad were channeling more things to write about for the story of his family.

Windhill Farms takes you back in time to the 1940s when life was simpler. The journey begins with a young family traveling in Pennsylvania in search of a farm to purchase. The story tells of the struggles they have in fixing up an old dilapidated farmhouse and also how Van (the author's father) supported his family as an illustrator in the 1940s and 50s. The journey also tells about the conflicts between mother and daughter as the mother had two more children late in her life and her older daughter was taking care of them.

Let this wonderful story take you on "Van's journey" as the family evolves around their life in the country.

Special thanks go out to my dear friends:
Jill Gray, Donna Sleight, Susan Bianculli,
Trish Hawkins and Lorraine Watkins,
for encouraging me to write this book
and the desperately needed help they
gave me with editing.

Chapters

Chapter 1

Fog Makes Driving Miserable

It *was November, 1939 and most of the trees were bare of their leaves, but the ones that were left rained down along the country roads, swirling around in the light breezes of Fall. My family and I traveled along Highway 17 through New York and on into Pennsylvania in our trusty green 1936 Oldsmobile. My name is Earl C. Van Swearingen, but most people just called me 'Van.' My wife Margret, and I had been married for fifteen years by this point, and we had a twelve-year-old daughter named Barbara. We were a close-knit family who enjoyed taking trips to the country, and it was our first time heading to this part of the Keystone State. I was fortunate, being in my mid-thirties and having a successful freelance business as an illustrator. This career allowed me to take time off from work when I needed it. Margret's father had just died in October and she was not completely over it.*

Margret, a petite woman with short auburn hair, looked out the car side window from time to time. "What on earth do people do here?" she wondered aloud.

I too, wondered, as the towns in upstate New York and Pennsylvania were small and didn't have much around them but countryside and small farms.

To amuse herself, my daughter would come up with romantic stories of people living in some of those towns as we passed through them. "Ahh... he was in love with the librarian and they met under the apple tree," she would invent dramatically. "It was love at first sight!"

"Oh Barbara," Margret would sigh in response. "You sure do come up with some wild stories."

Pouting a little, Barbara would subside for awhile.

After one of these exchanges, I noticed that fog was beginning to creep in around the mountains and that the sun was slowly going down, making the roads harder to see. I hadn't realized how late it was as my mind had been on the work that needed to be done. I had recently been illustrating stories for magazines, plus a special illustration for *Colliers*, and both projects had deadlines before the end of the month. But now it was time to start thinking about a place to stay overnight.

"I'm hoping we can find a tourist room or cabin soon, but it's really hard to see anything with this thick fog," I said as I continued driving on the winding roads. "Keep a look out, everybody, and let me know if you see anything."

Moments later Barbara's long dark hair whipped in the breeze as she rolled down the window for a better look at the road ahead.

"Look!" she exclaimed. "Look! I can see a welcome sign for *Appalachian Cabins!* There! I can see it up ahead!"

About half way up the road we could see the ghostly outline of a farmer's house, and I stopped the car at the bottom of the bumpy drive that led to the building. No cabins were to be seen in the growing dark, despite the sign's promise.

Margret was less cautious about the situation and more concerned about staying warm because the outside temperature was starting to drop.

"Go check it out, Van," she urged. "We'll wait here in the car."

I ventured up toward the house. To my surprise, a man's cheery voice greeted me from a side porch. He was a tall and slender elderly man and in overalls, a plaid jacket and a wool hat.

The man stepped off the porch and said, "Well, hello there. Looks like you folks might need a place to stay. I'm Mr. Adams and I own the place."

"Yes, we do," I replied. "We're hoping you have a cabin for us to rent until morning."

"Ellen, come on out here," he yelled to someone inside the house. "These folks need a place to stay."

Mr. Adams evidently assumed we would be taking one of the cabins, as the still invisible Ellen lit up the row of lights that illuminated the outsides of some remarkably well kept cabins that were behind the farmhouse.

"Just a moment, I want to drive my car up," I said before walking back down the hill. I had been a little reluctant to take something sight unseen, but after the lights were on, I'd become more excited about what we'd found on that dark foggy night. When I got back to the car, Margret rolled down the window and shivered as she asked, "Well, do we have a place to stay tonight?"

"Wait until you see!" I replied almost as cheerily as Mr. Adams's greeting had been.

I drove us up to the cabin where a woman of Amazonian proportions with rosy cheeks, gray hair and wearing a man's hat and heavy sweater, stood waiting to show us where to park. We saw smoke coming out of the chimney and the warm glow of the lights inside through the curtains as Mr. Adams got the place ready for us. We eagerly got out of the car when the front door opened.

"Come on in!" Mr. Adams motioned us to join him.

We wasted no time climbing the steps to the small front porch and following him as he led us inside to the fireplace to thaw out. The woman from outside came in after us and introduced herself as Mrs. Adams.

"We're the Van Swearingens," I said, introducing my family. "This is my wife Margret and my daughter Barbara. I'm Earl, but friends call me Van."

"So very glad to meet you," Mrs. Adams acknowledged.

The cabin looked like a little hunting lodge with its rustic wood siding and tongue and groove walls inside, and the atmosphere inside was a complete change from the gloom outside. We were shown two small bedrooms with a bathroom in-between them consisting of a shower, a toilet and sink with hot and cold running water. The large, single front room with a kitchen area and a small wood cook stove on one side and the furnished living room on the other side, completed the tour. Margret and Barbara were quite taken with the big log-burning fireplace with its wide mantel full of knick-knacks. It was quite nice for an overnight rental.

While I unloaded the bags from the car in the chilly, damp night, Mr. Adams brought in a huge pile of firewood and placed it by the fireplace. He then carefully placed two more logs on the fire.

"Are the logs included in the rental cost of the cabin?" I asked as I backed up to the fireplace to get warm again.

"Yep," answered Mr. Adams. "Burn as much as you like."

I was relieved. I was well aware of how much it would cost to buy firewood back in our hometown of Rye; it was probably more than the rent for the cabin would be.

Mrs. Adams went and got the registry book and I had to go through what had become the regular procedure of spelling Earl C. Van Swearingen for her. "So what is the cost for the cabin?" I asked.

"Two dollars," Mrs. Adams answered.

Smiling because I had been right about the cost, I handed her two dollars which she put in the side pocket of her sweater. Mrs. Adams proceeded to make herself at home in the cabin by sitting in a big stuffed chair near the door.

"Is there anything else that ya might need? Is everything all right for you folks?" she asked.

Margret came forward and said, "Everything is just fine, but I would love a nice cup of hot tea!"

"Well, Mr. Adams can go to the house and fetch ya some tea and milk. Milk is twelve cents per quart." Mrs. Adams then told her husband, "Tom, would ya also bring 'em cookies I baked this afternoon."

Mr. Adams stood up from where he was crouched next to the heat. "You folks just stay warm by the fire. I'll be right back."

"So tell me about you folks." Mrs. Adams asked, "Where did ya say ya'r from? How long ya been married?"

"Van and I met at McKinley High School in Canton, Ohio," Margret answered. "I guess you would say we were high school sweethearts. Van

14

graduated a year ahead of me, but after I graduated, we got married in May of 1925. Our daughter was born in 1927 in Canton." Margret continued, "We moved to New York City just before the Great Depression hit in '29 and from 1929 to 1931 we lived in several different places. One exciting place was Buenos Aires, Argentina, where Van worked with J. Walter Thompson Advertising Agency as their Art Director. We also traveled to England through his job with JWT, but while we were there the agency sent us back to the US because of the War and also the Depression. When we arrived back in the states, of course the Depression was in full force."

I was a little apprehensive about adding to my wife's story, since she seemed to be enjoying bragging about our travels. I decided to just let her talk.

Mr. Adams arrived back with tea bags, milk and a tin of oatmeal cookies. Mrs. Adams had the kettle on the stove hot and ready and she made a pot of tea for us. She poured a cup of tea and handed it to Margret and another cup for me. Barbara poured herself a small glass of milk. My wife kept on talking. "Van was able to get a job teaching magazine illustration with the Grand Central School of Art in New York City. He does a lot of illustrations for magazine stories. We're now renting a house in Rye, New York, but would like to find a house that we could buy as our country home. I've inherited some money from my father who died recently and we think buying a farm would be a good investment."

"My goodness, you folks have been to a lot of places, and I'm sorry to hear 'bout ya father," Mrs. Adams said. "I must admit, I haven't been anywhere but here. I married my hired hand after my first husband had passed. I couldn't understand why he wouldn't take my name since everyone knew my farm as the Tate Farm." She laughed a little but Margret just stared at her as that was a new angle of thinking for her. I tried not to laugh as I listened and watched the two ladies.

I leaned towards Mr. Adams and asked, "Are there many animals left in the woods these days?"

"Oh yeah, we got plenty of deer in the area. If it weren't so foggy I'd drive you up through the field and we'd probably see twenty or thirty deer eating apples from under the trees," Mr. Adams replied.

I didn't believe his statement so I quickly challenged him. "My car has a good spot light on it, how about us taking my car and drive up there right now?"

"Well, it's purty foggy," he said hesitantly.

"I don't mind a little fog."

I had convinced Mr. Adams to show me the deer in the orchard.

"Would you like to see some deer?" I asked my family as I got ready to go.

Margret was enjoying the warm cabin too much to even think about going, but Barbara jumped up to grab her coat.

"I would love to go along! I've only seen deer in a zoo!" she said enthusiastically.

We were headed out to my car when Mr. Adams spoke up. "Wait a minute folks, let's take my pickup truck. My truck is older than yours and I drive these dirt roads and fields all the time and know where the ditches are."

I was glad he made the offer since I had previously ripped a rear fender on a rock trying to drive through a field on a different country trip. It was quite an adventure bouncing around in Mr. Adam's truck as we headed up through one of the corn fields. The corn had been cut, leaving stubble all over the field. We detoured around wet spots, stones, and rocks. All of a sudden Mr. Adams slammed on the brakes, throwing us toward the windshield.

"What was that for?" I gasped.

Mr. Adams pointed out the windshield, and I spied a small animal with two little balls of fire for eyes peering at us right in front of the car. It dashed away into the fog after a moment.

"That was a skunk," Mr. Adams chuckled. "I thought maybe I'd better not hit him."

We had just started again when a similar animal jumped in front of the truck causing us to stop abruptly again. "Another skunk," he muttered. He had no more than put the truck in gear again, when he pointed, "Look ahead!"

There was a group of ten or twelve deer running about fifty feet in front of us and bounding away fast. My first impression of them, however, was of a number of tails flopping like those big bunny rabbits.

"Oh Daddy, look at the deer!" Barbara said as she sat up straight in the seat. "They're everywhere!"

We made several runs into different parts of the apple orchard and in the end had rounded up twenty-five or thirty deer and chased them into the woods above the orchard away from the fruit trees. My daughter didn't stop laughing excitedly until Mr. Adams drove us back to our cabin. By this time I was cold enough that the lights inside the cabin looked inviting.

When I opened the car door, Barbara squealed a little at the coldness of the wind which followed us as we scurried up the porch stairs and into the cabin. I shut the door firmly while Barbara ran up towards the warmth of the fireplace.

"Oh Mom, you should have seen all the deer!" she said excitedly. "We even saw some skunks!"

"Oh my," said Margret worriedly, "I hope the skunks stayed far away!"

"Sure, we gave them plenty of space," I said reassuringly.

"Well, thank you so much Mr. Adams for taking us to see all the deer," as I started for the door to hold it for them. "I guess we'll let you go and we'll see you in the morning."

Taking the hint, Mrs. Adams rose up from the comfort of the chair to join her husband.

"Good night and if you need anything, just let us know," Mr. Adams said pleasantly as they slowly closed the door behind them on their way out.

When they were gone, we started unpacking just enough things to get ourselves ready for bed. The fire made the cabin cozy and warm after a long day on the road. We were too tired to think about supper, but did eat a few of the cookies and drank some milk.

"I'm going to bed," Barbara announced.

"Well, give us a kiss good-night!" Margret said.

Barbara kissed her mother, "I love you Mom."

"Love you too," Margret responded. "Have a good sleep."

"Night Daddy," and gave me a kiss and hug.

"Love you and don't let the bed bugs bite." I said jokingly.

The room was quiet except for the crackling of the fire. We looked at each other and both got up off of the couch, turned the lights out in the living room and headed for bed.

"Goodnight honey," I said and gave her a kiss. We were both tired and ready for a goodnight's sleep.

"Goodnight, Van," Margret replied and turned the light out.

The next morning we were awakened by something either dropping or being thrown onto the metal roof of the cabin.

"What on earth is that?" Margret wondered as she got up to look out the windows.

The sun was just coming up and she could see the mountains clearly as the fog had burned away.

I walked out onto the porch and looked up to see an apple tree branch hanging over the cabin. It was the fruit that was dropping to make a loud clink clank on the roof. By the time Barbara finally got up and dressed, I had made a fire in the cook stove and Margret had heated water for tea. I had brought in the semi-dry rolls from the car that we had purchased at a delicatessen the day before, plus we still had some of the oatmeal cookies left. I added some of the apples that had made it to the ground, and I must admit we felt like we had a wonderful breakfast.

"I would like us to get on our way so we can do a little more sightseeing." I said as I was putting our suitcases by the door.

"I think we need to just take it easy and enjoy the morning here," Margret suggested as she

20

looked out at the beautiful view of the mountains. "It's so peaceful here."

I agreed, so we stayed to explore the farm. The three of us picked up more apples as we walked, and the scenery around us had my wife and I talking about having a place of our own in the country.

"It might be fun to have a farm to go to on vacations or even on weekends," I said.

"I think it would be wonderful to live up here," Margret responded. She was becoming excited about this new idea, "a place we could really call home."

Neither Margret nor I had ever lived on a farm. I had spent time on my uncle's farm one summer as a teenager, and I loved it.

"I would love to live on a farm and we could even have horses!" Barbara said as she picked up apples from the ground and placed them in an old basket she had found beside the cabin. "Look at all the apples, Daddy!"

The morning passed quickly and it was time to leave. Just as we had gotten all our things together and were about to pack up the car to head back to Rye, Mr. Adams stopped by our cabin.

"Take as many apples as you would like!" he said as he picked a couple more and placed them in the nearly full basket. "Looks like you've got a bushel of apples already."

"Thanks, these are delicious!" I said as I bit into one. "You've got a lot of apple trees here. Do you sell them?"

"Yeah, we take a lot of them to some of the groceries and farmer's markets nearby. Yep, looks like we'll have a really good crop this year." He picked up an apple and looked at it and took a bite.

"Well, my family and I really appreciate your hospitality, Mr. Adams, and we'll be on our way in a few minutes."

I put our suitcases in the trunk of the car. Margret and Barbara got into the car and as I slid into the driver's seat and started the engine, we said our good-byes and waved out the car windows.

"You folks stop by anytime." Mr. Adams called back cheerily.

We drove off and began looking at farms down the road and wondering how much a forty or sixty acre farm would cost.

After driving for a while, we saw a road sign that enticed us to stop and have lunch. While we were eating, we discussed what it might be like to live on a farm. When we finished lunch it started to rain. We got back in the car when I noticed the fuel gauge was getting low, so the next stop was the gas station down the road.

While the gas attendant was filling up the car, I asked him, "How would a farmer go about purchasing a farm around here?" I didn't want to let on that we were city folks and I didn't want to seem ignorant about farms.

"If you stay on this route, you'll be going through Towanda, Pennsylvania, within the next forty miles," the young gas attendant replied as he cleaned my windshield. "Why not stop in and see Mr. Fanning at the Federal Land Bank of Baltimore? He should be able to fix you up with most anything."

Following his advice, we drove about an hour in the drizzling rain. We slowed down each time we saw a cute farmhouse or an old barn with cows grazing in the fields nearby, which fueled our ambition about having our own farm.

"Look, Mom!" as Barbara pointed at some goats in a field. "Aren't they cute? Oh, can we have some goats if we get a farm?"

"That might be a good idea," I replied. "The goats can keep the grass down."

"I want a horse too!" Barbara demanded. "Maybe we can get a couple of horses so you can ride with me. Okay, Daddy?"

"Let's first see if we even find a farm to buy." I reminded my daughter.

We arrived in Towanda and hurriedly found the bank. I parked the car and, leaving my wife and daughter in the car, ran through the pouring rain to the front doors. I got soaked before getting inside, but I didn't let that deter me from finding out where the Land Bank office was. I was directed up a narrow stairway to the second floor and soon met Mr. Fanning.

"Hello, my name is Earl Van Swearingen," I introduced myself as I held out my damp hand. I was a little embarrassed by the way I must have looked. I was sure Mr. Fanning thought I was not a prospective buyer, but he was courteous and shook my hand.

"I'm interested in finding a farm to buy in this area," I continued. "My family and I live in New York right now, but would love to find a place out this way. We're on our way back to New York today. Is there anything you can do to help us?"

"I've got a couple of listings for farms that you could stop and look at on your way back to New York," he said, and scooped up a list off his desk to hand to me.

"Oh, this is great! Thanks. You might be hearing from us again," I said happily. We shook hands again and I made my way back down the stairway.

After getting wet a second time dashing back to the car, Margret and Barbara looked at what was on the paper and were curious enough to want to take a look at some of the properties if they weren't too far off the main road.

"This is exciting!" said Barbara as she read the information on two of the listings. "This weekend has been a real adventure."

"I believe our adventure is just beginning!" said Margret as she looked at the listings and read the directions to the closest one.

We soon came to an intersection and after a slight hesitation, we started up the dirt road that turned off from the main road. The car slipped every which way.

"We can do this!" I said encouragingly while gritting my teeth.

"Maybe we should turn around and go back," Margret pleaded.

"There isn't any place to turn around. We'll just have to keep going."

It must have been a mile and a half from the paved road before we came to the farm and looked at it eagerly through the car windows. It had been abandoned for some time and the former tenant, or someone, believed in taking everything with them. There wasn't a window or window sash left in the house, and the front porch had fallen off. But in our delirium for farms we found it quaint and liked it anyway.

"We can put it back together," I said, ignoring the rain.

I went out to the barn and found it in surprisingly good shape. Margret and Barbara followed me inside despite getting wet as well.

25

"Oh wow!" said Barbara as she looked around, "We could have a lot of horses in here!"

"This barn could be insulated and made into a large studio," I suggested studying the space. "I could cut a hole up there," I pointed to the roof, "and glass it in. I could have more light over there by cutting a window and have the northern light filter in. I can't believe the price of this entire parcel of one-hundred-twenty acres is only twelve hundred dollars," I said as we left the barn.

Though we were all soaked from the rain, we continued to inspect the rest of the out-buildings, which included a building that was probably used for storage, a small chicken barn and a smaller barn. I went back inside the dilapidated house and got my small notebook out of my jacket and drew a floor plan while making notes. The farm would only be a summer home for us for a few years, until we got things rebuilt.

"We would need to redo the kitchen and put in a bathroom," said Margret as we checked out the empty rooms of the old farmhouse. "Nothing is left, no appliances, toilet, sinks, nothing!"

We went outside and looked out over the land. "The only thing that I don't like is that it is located down in a deep valley," I observed. "I would rather have wide open spaces. The location is somewhat depressing, but after all, what could one expect for what they're asking?"

We got back in the car to leave and almost got stuck in the mud when we tried to turn around. When we were finally able to churn our way out of it, we found that the tracks we'd made on the way in made it easy to get back to the main road. We drove nearly a hundred miles to Scranton before we stopped briefly to eat, and then drove on to our home in Rye, talking and discussing farms almost all the way home.

The "bug to own a farm" had bitten us.

Chapter 2

We Bought A Farm

We spent many evenings during that early winter of 1939 in Rye tearing pictures and articles from House & Garden and farm magazines and pasting them in a scrapbook. Margret got a couple of quite interesting books from the library on farming, and I bought a Farmers Bulletin on subsistence farming which I read and reread until I knew it by heart.

The week before Christmas was mild with no snow on the ground in Rye, so we decided to pack our bags and blankets and head for Towanda to make the purchase. I threw in some extras like hand tools, some rope, and a hatchet, just in case we got stuck again on some mountain road. When we arrived in Towanda and parked at the land bank office, the three of us marched upstairs to meet with Mr. Fanning. He had not been expecting us but was once again politely accommodating.

"We would like to make a down payment on the farm that you told us about a month ago." I went through a description of the farm to the last detail to show we'd been there.

"I'm sorry folks, but that farm was sold only a week or so after you were there," said Mr. Fanning regretfully. "I'm truly sorry."

"Oh no!" I said as I couldn't believe our dream farm was sold! "Are you sure?"

"I'm quite sure and again, I'm sorry."

Margret and Barbara were also upset and stunned by such news as I could see the tears welling up in Margret's eyes.

"All of our plans and dreams." Margret said as she grabbed my arm, "I can't believe we just lost our dream farm. What now?"

I was stunned, but tried not to show it. "Everything happens for a reason and it was evidently not meant for us to have it," I said in a positive manner to buck their spirits up.

"Maybe one of these will be what you're looking for?" Mr. Fanning said as he handed me a listing of fourteen more farms in Bradford County, several of which were within our price range.

I thanked him and then we went over to the courthouse to get a detailed map of the county so we could check the listings. There, we learned that the only maps that they had were framed and hanging on the walls.

"Go across the street and see if maybe the printer has some smaller maps for sale before he closes up shop," advised the clerk.

Margret and Barbara went back to the car and waited while I dashed over to printer's shop and successfully bought a map for twenty-five cents just before he closed for the day. On our way to Towanda, we had noticed a good looking tourist home near Wysox called The Rose House, about two miles down the road, so we stayed there for the night. It was a nice accommodation and the owners were helpful with information about the area that we would be exploring.

The next morning, we set out with our map and listings looking for the perfect farm. The first one that sounded good was thirty-six miles from Towanda, close to a town called Montrose. During the drive, the morning got colder and cloudy overhead, but we kept on driving. We found the farm and it was very much to our liking, but was a thousand dollars more than we had planned to pay.

"Oh well, that's okay, it's really not what we're looking for," Margret convinced herself as we drove on.

The next one on our list was another twenty-eight miles over secondary roads towards South Warren. When we got there we saw a square box-like house with all of the front windows knocked out and no barn in sight.

"Nope, that's not it," I said as we turned around and drove on.

The next farm didn't appeal to us either and left us facing a drive of about sixty miles to the next one on the list near a town called Checkerville. I drove as fast as I could on these mountain roads since it was getting late in the afternoon. At first, we had trouble finding that farm, and we drove up and down mountain roads until we were about to give up. Finally, we stopped at a house sitting on the top of a mountain. The wind was blowing at a terrific rate and we wondered why the house hadn't toppled over. We were cold, but I got out of the car and leaned into the wind until I reached the door. I was almost sure the place would blow away before someone came to the door, but then another car drove up and out piled a lot of people. I didn't know who they were or where they came from, but the door was soon unlocked and everyone, including myself, pushed into the house out of the wind.

"Ah, hello, I'm looking for a farm that's in this area that's for sale," and took the piece of paper that listed the farm.

While one of the men started a fire in the wood burning cook stove, another man came over to me and looked at the listing. I quickly glanced around and the place was in shambles.

"You found it, this here is the farm," he announced with a chuckle. "You goin'na buy this here place?"

"I don't think so," I answered, making my way back towards the door. "Sorry to have bothered you."

I hurried back to the car and we crossed that farm off of our list in a hurry. As we left, it began to snow and slowed down our driving in the mountains.

"Let's just go home," Margret suggested, the worsening weather dampening her enthusiasm; Barbara agreed.

"Wait a minute! We only have two more farms to look at," I pleaded as I looked at the list again. "Come on, it wouldn't feel right if we returned home without looking at the last two farms, even if we have to look at them using our flashlights."

At the town of Wysox, we took an abrupt turn north toward Windham Center, another sixteen miles. The two farms listed were located some twenty miles off the main road from that small town.

"Oh Van, this is crazy!" Margret complained. "It's cold and getting dark and we don't know where we're going."

"I'm sorry, but we need to keep going." I said firmly as I kept driving.

I felt bad about the whole affair as well as my original idea of looking for a farm right in the dead of winter, but that wasn't stopping me. It continued snowing for some time, but when the sky cleared and the moon came out we could see the houses and fields quite clearly. We came into what we thought was Windham Center and started up the road where we believed the farm, with its two-hundred-plus acres of land, was located. To our surprise, the road ended in a steep pasture. After some maneuvering, we got the car back on the road and drove down to the corner store. We all got out of the car and quickly went into the store to get warm.

"Is this Windham Center?" I asked the storekeeper standing behind the counter.

"I reckon it is," as a big bashful smile crossed his lean face. "I'm the owner, Mr. Dutton. Come on in and get warm."

The store reminded me of all the storybook country stores with its shelves filled with can goods and other grocery items. The wide wood plank floors squeaked as I walked across the room and the counter top had jars of honey and homemade jams. The shelves below it were full of colorful jars of hard candy and chewing gum. I also noticed a glassed in area with sweet-rolls and sticky-buns and I could smell fresh coffee brewing.

Toward the back of the store a big cast iron stove was the main attraction. I noticed a big rough looking old fellow sitting behind it chewing tobacco. As we approached the stove, he lunged forward and deftly opened the little door in the side of the stove. He made a perfect shot inside with his tobacco spit, and the embers in the wood fire sizzled.

He looked up with a quizzical look on his face, but all he said was, "Ya folks look kinda cold." He pulled an end of the bench towards the stove, indicated that Margret and Barbara should sit and get warm.

My wife and daughter lost no time in making themselves at home around the stove, while I bought some sticky buns and bars of chocolate from the storekeeper and opened the packages for my family. We must have been some sight because the third man, a tall lean looking fellow, studied us from the other side of the stove and the storekeeper's wife appeared from the back room with a big questioning smile on her face.

"My goodness, welcome to our little store," she announced. "I'm Rose Dutton. Are you folks lost?"

"We're not sure," I answered. "Does anyone know where the Krause Farm is located?"

My hopes dropped a bit at the blank looks on their faces. It was obvious the name didn't mean anything to anyone there. Despite that, I pulled out the slip of paper that had been given to me at the Land Bank office and read out a full description of the farm. There were sufficient clues in this description to prompt recognition by one of the men who was sitting nearby.

"Why, that's the Shoemaker Farm. Oh wait, I do remember now, a family by the name of Krause did live there for a few years, but that was ages ago."

The old fellow introduced himself as Mr. Hoople. He proceeded to give me the history of the place and how to get up there in the morning. But waiting that long didn't suit me; I wanted to go up and see it right then and there. I asked if he'd be willing to take me there. He initially said 'no,' but Mr. Hoople finally agreed to go with me as I persisted in asking. Margret and Barbara decided to remain at the store where it was warm.

"Great! Let's go!" I said as I practically pulled the man to the car while he continued to protest the night, the time of year and the cold.

With Mr. Hoople's directions, we went back up the road I'd gone up before, but he directed me to turn off onto a road that I'd missed in the twilight. I drove past a couple of barns and farmhouses and crossed over a narrow bridge and further down the road he directed me to turn onto a short steep dirt drive.

Mr. Hoople said, "Well, here it is, this is it."

The moon lit the snow covered surroundings. I could see a two-story farmhouse and a couple of barns with the dirt road disappearing into the distance beyond them. I felt I could have made dozens of sketches of what I wanted to find, but didn't believe any of them would have come up to my expectations as closely as this old dilapidated place. From the backseat of the car I handed Mr. Hoople one of my flashlights and I took the other. I rushed in to explore the house, dashing through the kitchen, dining room, and living room. Slowing down, I walked up the narrow staircase to find one large bedroom, two small ones and a hallway running between them. Glass had been knocked out of the windows and the wind blew freely throughout the place.

"Isn't this place wonderful!" I exclaimed as I went back down the stairs to where Mr. Hoople was waiting.

"Well, I think you'd need to buy a good house that won't need so many repairs," Mr. Hoople said doubtfully as he rubbed his hands together in an effort to warm them.

During the exploration, the parlor door blew closed with a bang! Mr. Hoople reached for the knob and that was when we discovered there wasn't one on that side of the door.

"We're locked in!" I said with dismay. I went and tried to open one of the windows, but none of them budged. Coming back to the door, I looked at the latch, and then asked Mr. Hoople, "Now what do we do? Got a pen knife?"

Mr. Hoople felt around in his pocket and handed me a knife. I took it and fumbled with the lock, expecting to unscrew it and take it off. It still wouldn't come off since the screws were stripped.

Finally, in desperation, I inserted the blade of the knife in the lock and turned it. The door latch opened and that's all there was to it. We could get out.

"Come on. Let's get outta of here, before we get inta any more trouble!" Mr. Hoople said as he went eagerly out the door towards the car.

"Just a minute," I yelled back, and I dashed up to the barn. It seemed to be in better condition than the house, but I couldn't tell much about it with just a flashlight. But the cold led me in to keeping it a short inspection.

When we got back to the car, Mr. Hoople started blustering, "Ya must be crazy to be wantin' to see this place on a freezing cold night! And I musta been crazy to have brought you here. Come on, get us back to the store where it's warm."

When Mr. Hoople and I finally got back, Margret and Barbara looked content and comfortable sitting by the stove with their hands wrapped around mugs of hot tea.

"I believe I've found the farm!" I said with excitement to them.

"That's nice, dear," said Margret, sipping her tea.

"Another sticky bun?" asked Barbara, waving one in my direction.

I felt a little put off at the slight attention to my announcement from my family, but I took the sticky bun from my daughter and settled down to getting warm again.

"I'll be saying goodnight," said Mr. Hoople. "It's been an exhausting evening."

"Thanks for taking me up to the farm," I said gratefully. "I hope we'll meet again."

An indistinguishable grunt was his reply as he left the store.

"Let's drive back to the tourist home near Wysox," I suggested to Margret. "We can come back in the morning and I'll show you the farm."

On the drive back to Wysox, I told them about the farm, rambling on about it until we got back to the Rose House. I was so excited, that I had a hard time sleeping that night. We left for the farm early the next morning, and when we pulled up to the farmhouse, I was gratified that my family's first reactions to the farm mirrored what mine had been.

"Oh wow!" Barbara said as she got out of the car, "Look at this place! Oh Daddy, I love it!" She ran up to the front door and twirled around on the porch in excitement.

Margret kept quiet as she studied the house. She finally said, "It does have possibilities and I love the view. Let's go inside."

Daylight revealed that most of the plaster was off the walls and an empty wasp nest hung from the ceiling in the living room.

I said, waving all that aside, "The walls and ceiling can be plastered and fixed easily."

Margret and Barbara began to visualize the house fully decorated and furnished.

"We can put the table over here and the sofa can go over there," Barbara commented "And oh I love the big bay window!"

"The kitchen needs some work," Margret noted. "We'll need to get a stove and refrigerator and I'm not sure about the water situation and the sink in the kitchen. But more importantly, where is the bathroom?"

I was glad I'd brought our camera on this trip and went outside to take pictures of the house and barns. Most of the roof was off of the back of the house, but I observed that the lines of the supporting beams were still straight. But that was about all I knew to look for. The general style and lines of the house seemed to be quite authentic for the 1820's, when they built so many "lay on your stomach" windows in the upstairs front bedrooms.

"Bathroom? There is NO bathroom?" Margret questioned, coming around to meet me outback.

Turning around we saw...yes, an outhouse outside behind the house. We opened the door and saw two large holes in the wooden plank.

"Oh my, I'm not sure about this," Margret said as her eyes got bigger. She stared at the site and tried to imagine sitting there, "Nope, that's not going to happen."

Fortunately the barn was better. It had stanchions for eight head of cattle, though the silo beside it leaned considerably up hill. Besides the large barn, and several smaller buildings, which I didn't know what they were used for, there was an old horse barn across the road and maybe a tool shed. Having seen everything we needed to see, I made sketches of the floor plan of the house until my fingers were numb from the cold.

"Well, what do you think?" I asked, "Do we buy it?"

"Yes!" Margret and Barbara said eagerly.

We got back into the car and drove to Towanda, hoping we could meet with Mr. Fanning of the Land Bank office that afternoon. Mr. Fanning, once again, was nice and agreed to meet with us without an appointment. When we told him we wanted the farm, he pulled out the proper file and wrote the necessary papers while we wrote out a check for one hundred dollars as a down payment for the two thousand dollar farm. Signing everything needed took considerable time, but after everything was finished the agent said, "Well, I wish you and your family luck and I guess I won't need these photographs anymore."

He handed me two photographs of a house and a sketch of the farm boundaries from the farm's folder.

One photo looked like the farm that we had purchased, but the other was definitely not. I handed him back the other photo, "This must have gotten into the files by mistake."

Mr. Fanning took it from me, but said, "I'm sure this is a picture of the house on that farm," Mr. Fanning said, "I checked up on it myself about six months ago."

"Well then," I said "I am afraid you have sold us the wrong farm. We saw no house that looks like this photo."

I momentarily wondered if I had been swindled, but Mr. Fanning looked far from being a swindling kind of man.

"Let me make you understand," Mr. Fanning said with a smile as he handed the photo back to me. "The picture I gave you is the main house. That's the one you saw. This second photo is of the other house on the property, which is the tenant house."

"We did not see a tenant house," I said puzzled.

Finally, Mr. Fanning convinced us that there was one further down the road past the house. We were quite surprised to find we had bought a farm, and a house, and also a house that we had never seen.

My wife and I looked at each other for a couple of moments, and finally said to each other, "What's another fifty miles? Let's drive back and see the second house we bought before we go home."

We went all the way back to the farm, drove past the main house, and soon found the tenant house. The joke was certainly on us. We had assumed when we had driven by that house earlier that it belonged to the adjoining farm. It goes to show how little we knew about the extent of two hundred and nine and a half acres.

"It looks like a little doll's house," Barbara said enthusiastically.

There were six rooms in the tenant house. One good size bedroom, a moderate size bedroom, and a small bedroom constituted the upstairs. Downstairs was a large kitchen, a small living room and what might be a bedroom or storage room off of the living room and an outhouse out back. This was not at all bad for something that we didn't know we had until the deal had been closed, despite the work that would need to be done to make it livable.

With the sketch of the farm boundaries in my hand, I went outside and looked up toward the top of the hill. Inspired by the fir trees in the woods, I announced, "You know what? I think that the woods up there must be ours, too. I'm going up there to get us a Christmas tree to take home. Christmas is only a week away."

Margret and Barbara were cold so they stayed in the car while I trudged up the hill with an ax and rope from the car. When I got up to the field beyond the barn, I began to doubt my wisdom and wished that I hadn't started after the tree. It was much farther than it looked and the snow was deep in the drifts which made walking difficult. Deer tracks were easily discernible in the snow and I wished that I could glide over it as they must have, marking the distance between hoof prints. The journey up the side of the mountain seemed endless. I was way beyond tired when I finally arrived at the cluster of fir trees.

Despite being exhausted at that point, I picked out a good Christmas tree nearby and cut it down without chopping off a foot. Tying the ax into the tree with the rope allowed me to have two hands to deal with dragging the tree back down the hillside. It wasn't such a job to drag the tree back because I could use my previous footprints to walk in, but to tie it on the car with the modern fenders and small running-boards, and to drive two hundred and twenty five miles with it back to Rye, was almost an art. We learned later that the paint worn off the fender from the tree rubbing against it on that trip cost several times the price of a good Christmas tree. We chalked the damage up to sentimental value, as it was the first tree cut from the first property that we'd ever owned, which made it an acceptable price to pay.

Chapter 3

Good Neighbors

In March of 1940, the week before Easter, the weather in Rye seemed like spring. Margret, Barbara and I decided to load up the car and head for our farm to start some repairs. The three of us squeezed into the front seat of the Oldsmobile because the rest of the car was taken up with tools and supplies: four rolls of roofing, glass for the windows, three camp cots, a camp stove, flashlights, a carpenters' toolkit, an ax, rope, household essentials, and a suitcase with some of our clothes. Tied down on top of the car was a large steamer trunk with blankets, sheets, pillows and more clothes.

"I hope we're not forgetting anything," I said after I shut the trunk for hopefully the last time.

As we left that morning, it really did feel like spring, until we got beyond the Catskill Mountains. From there, the snow was piled as high as the car on both sides of the road. The road was clear, but slippery.

"I don't know," Margret remarked uneasily. "I'm not sure this was such a good idea. It's snowing again and we're not even there yet."

"We've come this far," I said as I took my gloved hand and wiped the condensation from the inside of the windshield so I could see the road. "I'm hoping we can get there before dark."

We didn't make the trip to the farm in nearly the time we had expected to and arrived after dark. The side road to the farm was not plowed, but I tried it anyway. The car made it across the narrow bridge and then skidded in the snow until we were completely turned around.

"Oh Van, this is crazy!" Margret yelled. "We could all be killed trying to drive on this road!"

We made it back to the main road worrying that we might never get to the farm on this trip.

"Let's drive back to the tourist home where we stayed before in Wysox," I suggested.

We stopped in Wysox and had supper at a small café and talked about what we were going to do the next day and how we were going to get to our farm.

It was late when we arrived and we woke the owners of The Rose House. They were surprised to see us, but consented to let us stay for the night and got the beds ready.

"We're so sorry to inconvenience you, but we didn't know where else to go," Margret said as she and Barbara walked into the cozy room.

"Okay folks," the woman said. "I hope you'll have a good night's sleep."

She left and we got into our night clothes and went to bed. The next morning was cold, too cold to even think of driving back to the farmhouse and staying there without some kind of heat.

"You girls need to stay here," I suggested. I'll drive into Towanda and buy a sheet-iron wood-burning stove. I'll also need several lengths of stove pipe and a cross-cut saw. Plus I'll get some oil lamps."

"You be careful, Van," Margret said concerned. "The roads might still be bad and I would hate for you to get stuck somewhere and no one know that you're out there."

"I'll be careful," I reassured her. "I love you and I'll be back."

By the time I was finished shopping in Towanda, the car was completely loaded with all the material needed, even the seat beside me, so I drove back to Windham Center without Margret and Barbara. After inquiring at the general store we'd been to before, I learned that the road I had tried the previous night had still not been traveled.

"I don't think you could get to your farm with a car," said Mr. Barlow, the storekeeper. "You could approach it from the opposite direction." He gave me directions how to get there.

I set out over the more traveled creek road, which I found paralleled the road to my farm. I was able to drive for a mile or so before I came to an abrupt halt because of the snow. I gazed over my surroundings. To my left was a large farmhouse setting back from the road about a hundred feet. On the right was a smaller farmhouse, similar in style to our own house. I backed the car for a good start and then drove forward in low gear attempting to push through the snow. It was much deeper than it looked, and I got stuck up to the running boards. I gave the Oldsmobile the old one-two backwards and forwards, but the wheels spun with no traction.

Getting out, I took a good look at the rear wheels and noticed the deep snow packed around them. I wondered why I had tried such a foolish trick, especially without having put on the chains.

My wet gloves from trying to dig out some of the snow, made my fingers cold before I could unpack the chains, which were, of course, under all the stuff I had packed in New York.

"Sure is a cold morning," a young slender man with reddish hair said as he came from the direction of the farmhouse. "Bet ya could use some hep gettin' them chains on."

I was happy to see him. "I can definitely use some help," I said as I rubbed my gloved hands together. "My hands are so cold I can hardly feel them. My name is Earl Van Swearingen and I bought the farm up the road."

"Reynolds, Reynolds Carr is my name," he said as he grabbed the chain and stretched it out in the snow.

Within five minutes, another man and a grown boy came up to examine the situation. Both were tall and thin. They walked over and watched Reynolds get the chain set just right.

"Hi," I said as I introduced myself. "I guess you can see I need some help."

"I'm Ned Huddle and this here is my boy Donald. I live right over there and could hear ya talkin' and such and had ta see if we could help."

Without any prompting, they proceeded, bare handed, to put the chains on the car and back the car out of the drift. Then they invited me up to their house to get warm. Grace, Ned's wife who seemed to be the essence of kindness, scurried around the kitchen stove while verbally fussing over me.

She soon lifted a steaming kettle from the stovetop to pour a cup of coffee. "Come on over here and get ya'self warm young man. Here's you a cup of coffee and ya just sit yurself down and rest a minute."

"Thanks," I said gratefully as I wrapped my hands around the mug of coffee. "How far is it to the old Shoemaker farm from here? I just bought it and am trying to put a wood stove in before I go back to Wysox to get my family."

"It's jist up the road. That place adjoins our property," Grace said. "So where are ya from and why on earth would ya be tryin' to put in a stove this time of year?"

"We live in Rye, New York and when we left there, the weather was spring-like so we thought it would be nice to come and do some work on the place. I had no idea you still had snow up here."

A thin old man hobbled in with an arm load of firewood and introduced himself as "Dick." I later learned that Dick boarded and roomed with them, but not in the usual way. He actually made himself a part of the family.

Within the hour, all of us had gotten thoroughly acquainted and I felt I had always known the Huddles. We had quite a discussion about how to get to the farmhouse and finally decided to leave the car at the Huddles' and let Ned drive me up to my farm with his wagon and team of horses. We unloaded some of the woodstove items from my car and placed them on the wagon, since I needed to leave room for Margret and Barbara.

"Let me drive back to Wysox and get my wife and daughter," I said as I started for the door. "I know they must be anxious that I've been gone so long."

When I arrived back in Wysox, I explained to my family what had happened.

"Sounds like you had quite an adventure, Daddy." Barbara said while brushing her hair.

"I guess you could say that," I responded. "Let's get the rest of our stuff together and have a quick lunch somewhere in town and drive back to the Huddles."

"So who are these neighbors of ours?" Margret asked.

"Down to earth country folks that I'm sure you'll like," I said as we headed for the car.

"I guess we'll have to squeeze into the front seat again," Margret noted as she could see how packed the car was.

We ate at a small café in Wysox and afterwards headed for the Huddle's farm. It was only fifteen miles and I now knew the roads a lot better in the area.

I introduced Margret and Barbara to Ned, Grace and Donald. Barbara and Donald ended up eyeing each other, as they were about the same age.

Ned and Donald quickly hitched up the hay wagon and unloaded everything from the car onto the wagon, along with a few logs of firewood.

We got on top of the hay wagon. "Wow, this is exciting!" Barbara said as she climbed up on the wagon with help from Donald. "Thank you," she said to him, blushing a little at his kindness.

"Yur welcome," he replied, placing a blanket over her lap. "This here is to keep ya warm," he said before jumping down. He handed Margret a blanket and she sat close to Barbara as they huddled to keep warm. I just held onto the seat of the wagon as I watched Ned and Donald maneuver the team of horses.

Father and son walked beside the horses through the deep snow as the wagon inched ahead. At one place where the water from one of the fields ran over the road and made a frozen pond, we got stuck. Ned's expert handling of the horses got us out, and soon we could see our house over the rise in the road.

We had not rehearsed what to do at the farm, but we all quickly started doing the things at hand. Margret had the right idea as she suggested, "We need to first make one room as weatherproof as possible. That way we might be able to stay warm and dry. Let's put a sheet over the bay window to keep some of the wind out," she ordered. "Barbara, help me tack it up." The sheet bellowed inward from the wind, but it did help a little.

Barbara and Margret began to put the cots together and placed the bedding on them. They found an old wooden box that had been left behind and used it as a small table and brought in more items that Ned had unloaded from the wagon and placed in the empty kitchen.

Ned, Donald and I started setting up the stove. The pipe went straight up through a hole already in the ceiling in the living room, and we lined the hole with some kind of sleeve that the hardware man had suggested. Upstairs, the pipe continued up into a bedroom and then added short pieces of pipe to aim to the right and then a left into the chimney. The bottom of the chimney began about two and a half feet up from the bedroom floor, which was common in old homes in this area. After the stove pipe was up, we were all amazed to find only about fourteen inches of pipe left over. Usually, it happens the other way and you have to buy another piece of pipe.

The wood stove not only blushed, but got very red and hot all over, before I learned how to operate it properly. We put a metal bucket of snow on the top of the stove and before we knew it we had hot water for tea. It was nice to relax and marvel at all the work we had accomplished as we all sipped tea.

"I really appreciate all your help," I said. "I couldn't have done this by myself."

"That's what neighbors are fur," Ned replied and shook my hand. "You jus' let us know what you need. We'll be goin' now, but we'll come by again and see how yur doin.'"

Ned and Donald went back outside and turned their team of horses around and started back to their home. We stood by the door and waved. It suddenly seemed lonely when they yelled back, "We'll see ya folks tomorrow."

It had been a long day for us, I thought as it grew dark. Margret had purchased sandwich meat and bread and other groceries needed from the general store in Wysox and made sandwiches for our first supper at our farm. We were all tired and went to bed early in the same room on our cots as close to the stove as we dared.

"Goodnight, stay warm and I love you two." I said to Margret and Barbara as I kissed them both and crawled into my sheets and blankets on the squeaky cot.

"Love you too," Margret responded and covered her head with the blanket.

"Goodnight," Barbara said as she was almost asleep all wrapped up in her covers.

It was cold, so I slept fitfully to make sure I woke to put in more firewood every couple of hours to keep us from freezing. The sheets at the windows kept most of the wind out, but offered little protection against the real cold of the night. By morning we had burned most of the logs. I scurried around the barns and dragged in pieces of broken timber plus anything else that would burn.

"Come on," Margret said as she put bowls of cereal and milk on the steamer trunk being used as a table. "Let's eat some breakfast." She put pieces of a Hershey bar into some milk in a pot and heated it on the stove to make hot chocolate.

"Mom, what a wonderful idea," Barbara said as she sipped the hot chocolate.

"What's the plan for today?" Margret asked. "Looks like with all the building supplies you've got your work cut out for you."

"The first thing I want to do is cut glass to put in the big bay window. Old putty and tacks need to be dug out of the frames first, though," I said as I ate my cereal and drank some of the hot chocolate. "I'll have to build a ladder out of lumber that is lying around. It should be fine for putting in the top panes."

We went through the wood that had been salvaged from the fields and barns quickly, so a great deal of time was spent gathering more wood, even with a lot of help from Margret and Barbara. By late afternoon I had put glass in all of the living room windows and we were able to get the place quite warm.

"I'm wondering how I can find enough wood to keep the stove going all night." I pondered as I stoked the fire.

"Hello, anyone home in there?" a familiar man's voice yelled from outside, accompanied by the sounds of boots being stomped free of the snow on the porch.

It was Donald and Reynolds, who had come up to help us with anything that needed to be done. I told them about the wood situation.

Reynolds spoke up and said, "There's a telephone pole laying flat on the ground just down the road. We can cut that up and that should last you a long time."

We went down and carried the pole up to the driveway of the farmhouse and began sawing it up for fire wood. We would find out later that the big chunks of wood would solve the problem for quite awhile.

"Why don't ya folks come by our place later?" Donald suggested, as they walked down the driveway to the road after the sawing was done.

That evening after having soup and sandwiches again for supper, we walked down to the Huddles' farm by the light of the early-rising full moon and spent an enjoyable evening getting better acquainted.

"We weren't always farmers," Grace said at one point. "We used to be school teachers near Rome, Pennsylvania. Ned taught history and I taught home economics. Though we're first cousins, we fell in love, so we married and ended up having two children. Our Junia is in college right now studying to be a teacher, and you've met our son Donald."

"Both our children have bad eyesight," Ned explained. "Junia is able to wear thick glasses and she'll be okay, but Donald's eyes are much worse and he'll eventually go totally blind. Knowin' that, we decided to quit teachin' and buy a farm and teach Donald everything we could about farmin' and the lay of the land."

Grace said, with great pride. "Donald can do just about anythin' round here right now. His eyes are slowly fadin', but he can still see enough to get around."

"Yep," Ned agreed. "My only worry is him driving that tractor when he goes blind. I sometimes wonder, even now, if he sees well enough to know if somethin' is in the road like a dog."

"Now paw, I can tell when things are 'round me by the sounds," Donald spoke up. "I'm learnin' to use my other senses. Don't you fret."

Margret was looking around the large kitchen and noted the kerosene burning cook stove.

"Van, we need to get a stove like that for our kitchen. We have absolutely nothing in that kitchen. In fact it's just a big empty room with a sink and water pump!"

"That's something we need to think about," I interrupted. "We also need to figure out the well and pump so we can have water."

I began thinking of all the things that still needed to be done to the house.

"Come on, we need to get home and get some rest before starting work tomorrow," I said as I stood up. "Thank you again for all your help and being so neighborly."

"Well, ya folks get a good night's sleep," Grace said as she followed us to the back kitchen door. "Just a minute, let me get you some fresh milk and eggs." She scurried around the kitchen putting a bottle of milk, some lard, bacon and a carton of brown eggs in a basket to give us. "Now ya folks stay warm tonight."

"Oh my, looks like we're going to have a wonderful breakfast," Margret exclaimed. "Thank you so much!"

The night was clear when we went to bed, and since the room was warm, we all slept well. We also remembered from our camping days, that putting newspapers between the bed linen and the canvas of the camp cots made our beds warmer.

After having a real breakfast of bacon and eggs the next morning, the work began again, and each succeeding day became a repetition of the day before. Margret and Barbara helped by scraping out the old decayed putty and smoothing out the frames and I would carefully put the new panes in. In a couple of days, eighty-eight window panes had been installed with glazier's tacks, but no putty. This fixed most of the windows in the house and the whole house began to get and stay warm.

The warmth upstairs proved to have one disadvantage: there were plenty of holes in the roof where water had dripped in and frozen. That had left about a ton of ice piled up in the bedroom upstairs like an overgrown sand pile. As the room warmed up the ice began to melt and water dripped through the ceiling above the stove. The warmth also brought wasps crawling out of various places and we spent some time trying to kill them, but there were too many. We finally decided to let the wasps have the run of the ceiling and only took swats at them as a diversion from the rest of our work. Since none had attempted to sting us, it boiled down to a policy of live and let live.

The one room that we decided to make the most of was the living room. Margret had a knack for making things look homey, and she had it feeling like "home" in short order.

The three of us took breaks from work to do a little exploring from time to time. First we

checked out the horse barn on the other side of the road and found it had four large stalls and a loft for hay. At the far end was a large canvas cloth covering something bulky. When I pulled it off, we discovered an old horse-drawn sleigh. The seats were leather and a little worn with holes where mice made their nests or at least had taken the stuffing out of the seats. Old harnesses, bridles and other horse-related objects were discovered hanging from the walls with spider webs draping from one item to the next. "Now all we need is a horse to pull it," Barbara said happily as she checked the barn out.

Leaving the barn, we tried to calculate milking time at the Huddles' so that we could go over and get some more milk. Barbara and I decided to walk over there while Margret stayed behind to finish what she was working on. My daughter and I were gone about an hour, but when we arrived back we discovered Margret lying at the bottom of the stairs crying out in pain.

"Van, help!" Margret yelled out in pain.

"Where are you?" Barbara asked and found her mother lying on the floor at the bottom of the stairs.

"What happened?" I asked as I ran to her and carefully checked her out to make sure nothing was broken.

"I lost my balance and began falling and slid all the way down the steps on my back," she cried. "I didn't know how long you would be gone and I was afraid of trying to get up on my own. Oh, my back!"

"Here, let me help you to the cot," as I led her and carefully sat her down on the cot.

"I can't believe I fell down those stairs," she moaned as she slowly lay down to get comfortable.

Barbara made supper, but we didn't feel like eating. We were worried about Margret. My wife didn't want to go to the doctor because she thought she was only bruised and would be all right by morning. The next morning she did feel somewhat better, but walked with a great deal of pain. Barbara became a great help since Margret was unable to do any housework.

"Thank you Barbara," Margret said, "for taking care of me and the housework. I love you and appreciate you."

"Oh, Mom," Barbara responded. "I love you too and I want you to get better."

Since repairs had to continue, I moved on to contemplating the roof. I warmed up the rolls of roofing paper and laid them on the roof toward the back of the house where the boards were completely exposed. By evening, I had it covered in a "crisscross" fashion. At least I felt it would keep some of the weather out until summer.

That evening, with Margret feeling better enough to walk, we all went down to the Huddles.' Unfortunately, Margret slipped on some snow covered ice and fell hard again.

"I can't believe I fell again! Oh dear, I really do hurt." She limped her way to the Huddles' house and sat on the softest chair she could find during the evening.

"Here, let me get a pillow to put behind you," Grace said as she reached for a small pillow that was on another chair. "I'll get you some ice to put on your back to take the swellin' down?"

"Oh, maybe that would help," Margret moaned.

Grace got a chunk of ice and wrapped it in a linen towel and placed it between Margret's back and the chair. "Now how's that feel?"

"Oh, yes, I think this does help," Margret said as she repositioned it to the injured area of her back.

After getting Margret situated, I approached Ned who was sitting by the warmth of the stove. "I would like to make an arrangement with you

Ned. I would like it if you could clean out our well beside the house in the early spring and try to keep an eye on the place while we're gone."

"Sure, I can do that," Ned agreed. "How about I cut your yards and fields? I could use it for hay."

"That sounds like a great idea."

As the evening wore on, Margret's back began hurting again and it was with great effort that she walked the half-mile back to our house.

The next morning she felt worse and had a hard time moving around. "I just want us to go home to Rye," Margret requested. "I'll see a doctor when we get there. I want to be in my own comfortable bed."

"Okay, we can go ahead and leave now." I said soothingly. "We'll be home by dark."

Barbara and I hastily packed as Margret slowly made her way to the car. Many of our things were left about the house and we made no attempt to lock it, except for closing the doors securely against the weather. We stopped by the Huddles' to let them know the situation and said our good-byes. Most of the way home we talked of getting back to our house in Rye, so we could take a hot bath and get into a nice warm bed. Margret moaned when we hit rough spots in the road, but she tried not to complain too much.

When we finally arrived at our house it was cold, but our surprise came when we walked into the kitchen and found water all over the floor.

"Oh no, now what?" Margret cried out.

Suspecting what had happened, I ran upstairs to find the bathroom floor covered with water as well as part of the hallway. Two radiators had frozen and broken along with a water pipe in the bathroom while we were gone.

"I'll call the Hogans and see if we can stay overnight with them," I suggested.

"I can't believe this is happening to us," my wife moaned. "I just wanted to be in my own bed."

I called our neighbors across the street and told them what had happened, and they invited us to stay at their house for the night. We did get our hot baths and slept in comfortable beds that night, but it certainly was an imposition to place on any good friendship.

The next day, we called in a plumber and had the situation fixed and had the floors dried and cleaned up. We took Margret to the doctor's office, he was of the opinion that Margret's back was just bruised and it would take some time to heal, which was a relief to learn.

******

Towards the end of April and into May, I was very busy with my work while Margret healed and Barbara made herself useful about the house. I had several magazine illustrations to complete. Being a free-lance artist with deadlines to meet, I had little time to think of the farm. As an additional meal ticket, I had promised to teach a class on "Illustration" at the Grand Central Art School in New York City for the second year. My plans to get to the farm were delayed until school was out at the end of May. But then June came around and I undertook teaching a summer course on "Illustration" again at Grand Central Art School, requiring me to be in New York City for two days a week. I drove to the farm each week and returned for class every Wednesday and Thursday mornings. Margret and Barbara made these drives with me, so that all of our trips were delightful.

Before long, we gave up our rented home in Rye and had all of the furniture moved to the farm. Some of it had to be covered with canvas to keep it dry during the rains in the early summer.

My studio apartment in New York City was where I or we stayed when I had to be in the city for a few days. The apartment was small, but livable for the three of us and I could do some of my work there. The time we spent in the city depended on the illustrations I was working on and my teaching schedule. Most of my work I took to the farm to do. When there, my mornings were devoted to art, and I spent the afternoons doing repairs.

I ordered a kerosene stove called a Kerogas Stove from A.J. Lindemann Hoverson, out of

Milwaukee, wanting to start cooking and baking in our kitchen. Another expense was roofing supplies I ordered to fix our roof. It was going to be a busy summer.

Chapter 4
A Roof Over Our Heads

The Huddles had started a garden for us near the side of the house that spring of 1940. They planted corn, green beans, tomatoes, squash, lettuce and peas. We were spending most of our time at the farm that summer and it was nice having fresh vegetables from the garden.

"I've never had a vegetable garden to take care of," Margret said as she was pulling weeds. "It will be nice to have fresh vegetables all summer long."

"It was so thoughtful of the Huddles to do this for us," I said, as I helped pull out the unwanted greenery. "They're really wonderful neighbors."

"When do you think the roofing material will come?" Margret asked.

"It should be here any day. Then we'll have our work cut out for us." I stood up and stretched and looked at the house.

The next day we were thrilled that the kerosene stove was delivered. We both looked at the instruction book that came with it and did a fine job of putting it together.

"Guess I'll go ahead and light it," Margret said as she lit the burner.

We held our breath.

"Oh my goodness, it does work!" she said excitedly, as the flame caught and held steady.

It took some experimenting to operate it properly, but Margret learned with no great effort. It was nice having hot meals again with fresh bread and cakes from the oven.

The composition shingles for the house arrived a couple days later. It was time to get going with the much-needed roof repairs. I started tearing off the patchwork roofing I'd done last year in order to replace it with shingles. Margret decided to help with the roofing while Barbara cooked the meals. My dear wife spent some time on the roof with me a couple of mornings, but trying to keep up with the other duties of the house, the roofing became too much.

When I tore off sections of the old roofing, made of several layers of roofing paper over old hand wrought shingles, I discovered that not only were many of the old roof boards rotted, but the boards themselves had been spaced too far apart. That meant the repair, replacement, and realignment of everything, slowed down the work. When I finally put on the roofing material, I found that it was not as difficult.

"How's it going up there?" Margret called up around noon. "Do you want to take a break and have some lunch?"

"Sounds great!" I replied as I climbed down the ladder. "I need a break. My back is killing me."

"Sure hope you're not overdoing it," Margret said as she placed sandwiches and tomato soup on the table.

"I'm okay. I just wish it was done already."

"Barbara!" Margret shouted out the back door, "Lunch!"

"Coming," Barbara answered as she came across the field out back. "I picked some flowers." She put a bunch of daisies mixed with some pink flowers in a Mason jar with some water and placed it on the table. "I just love wild flowers."

"Oh, how sweet, I think those are wild roses," Margret said as she gently twirled the jar around to see them from all sides.

"I must say, I'm learning quickly how to do roofing," I said as I picked up another sandwich. "The wasps are hovering over me, but so far I haven't been stung or is it being bitten? Either way, they haven't really bothered me."

Late that afternoon, the roofing was completed over the main part of the house, but not the bedroom. That section had been prepared for roofing, but a sudden storm was brewing. I quickly placed an old canvas over the unroofed portion, but the wind ripped it aside. The rain came down hard as I tried to gather my tools and get inside.

"It's pouring and the rain is getting everything wet inside!" Margret shouted as she tried to salvage some items by moving some of the furniture to a dryer area. I moved some of the heavier furniture, but we didn't make it in time with the beds.

"Oh no, the bed is soaked and the rugs are saturated," Margret cried out! "Some of the water is running down onto the furniture in the parlor! I can't believe this is happening, just when we're almost done with the roofing and then this!"

"I know what you mean, it seems like we take a step forward and then something like this puts us back two steps." I looked around and saw all the water dripping off the beams above.

When the skies had cleared, we swept and mopped out the water and aired out the mattress and bedding in the sunshine.

"Are the cots that we brought last winter dry?" Margret inquired. "We can sleep on those since the mattresses are wet."

"I'll go check," I answered. I had stored them in the horse barn and brought them in. "Thank goodness, the cots are just fine. We can sleep on these tonight."

Over supper that night, Margret and Barbara had some ideas about remodeling the inside of the house. "We drew up some sketches of how it might look," Margret said, showing them to me.

"This just might work," I agreed as I studied the sketch. "But I think it might be time to hire someone else to handle it."

We hired Charlie Barlow, a recommended handy man, to implement our ideas while I continued with my repairs. A partition removed between the parlor and long bedroom gave us a larger parlor. Walls between two larger pantries were removed to give us a downstairs bedroom. This sounded simple enough, but the result was plaster on and in everything for most of the summer. Various windows and doors were taken out and moved about in the kitchen to give more wall space. Some of these operations may not have been justifiable, because after we removed the pantries we realized that we needed the pantries on a farm, especially since we didn't even have cabinets in the kitchen. We went ahead and had a local cabinetmaker build and install pine cabinets. Margret and Barbara painted the new cabinets an off-white, which made the kitchen quite charming.

The weather had been good during the late summer and recklessly I'd removed most of the old roofing on the rear "L" of the house. Of course, at the point when I'd had the most inner roof exposed; the weather had to turn. The wind picked up and dark clouds formed.

There was precious little we could do but to try to get the kitchen supplies and the dining room furniture moved as quickly as possible into the living room.

"It's really coming down!" Margret yelled out as we moved furniture.

"Here, put the table and chairs over here!" I yelled as I helped Margret with moving the table and placed it in the living room. "Barbara, grab that chair! Oh it's pouring!"

The rain came right through the ceiling, making even larger holes in the broken plaster.

Within half an hour, it appeared that the water would run over the door sill into the living room. I grabbed a brace and bit and bored holes in the kitchen and hallway floors with this hand drill to let the water run through into the basement. This worked well enough to keep the rain from flooding the living room, but it took almost a week of warm weather to dry out the house.

Roofing a house of that size turned out to be quite a job, but I had it finished by Fall. After doing the roof myself, I had Floyd Williams, who was said to be the best plasterer in the area, come over and plaster the various rooms where needed. On days when he came up to plaster he would have dinner with us, and Floyd became quite a good friend. He started bringing us a pail of honey on his visits, and he told us fascinating stories about his bees. He prevailed upon my sense of sportsmanship to get me to start a colony of bees. I could never have imagined anyone as interested in bees as he.

During one of our weekly drives back from New York City that Fall, we saw a severe storm far ahead of us. The past month had been quite dry and we hoped that some of that rain was falling on our farm. The rain started coming down hard. It was late afternoon when we stopped at the Windham Center Store to pickup some groceries and hurried inside.

Mr. Hooper ventured, "Looked like quite a blow up your way."

"Yes," I said. "We surely needed the rain."

"But," Mr. Dutton, the storekeeper, broke in, "it looked like a real blow!"

This made me a bit more serious about the matter and I hurriedly bought the supplies we needed and rushed off. The mud was too deep on the shortest road, so we went around to drive in on the Stateline Road that went by the Huddle's farm.

"Their place seems to be okay," Margret noted with relief.

"We'll let them know we're back," I said as I tooted the horn and continued on down the road not wanting to stop and chat.

A tree lay partly across the road not over 200 yards from the house. We were surprised at the size of the tree, but were able to make our way around it. When we reached the house, nothing seemed to be disturbed as the sun was going down over the mountain. Margret and Barbara put the groceries away and fixed a light supper. Afterwards, I read the local paper to catch up on the latest news in our area, and we went to bed.

The next morning when I looked out the bedroom window, the apple tree in which a dove had made a nest had disappeared!

"Oh my good God! I can't believe it!" I said, concerned. I immediately got dressed and put my boots on.

"What's going on?" Margret asked as she started to get out of bed in response to my words.

"We did have a bad storm yesterday. I need to go outside and assess the damage."

"Don't you want some breakfast first?"

"Not now, I need to see how things are outside. I hope the damage isn't too bad."

A quick look around the farm revealed that the roof of the smoke house had partially broken, and the chimney had fallen in. I noticed how the wild berry bushes did not fit against the barn anymore. They were in a dense mass standing over a foot from the barn. The barn itself had moved a foot and a half at one end, though only an inch or so at the other. Boards had fallen in here and there, leaving gaps in the walls and ceiling. Surprisingly, the storage barn 100 feet away had suffered almost no damage. I dashed up to the large cow and hay barn to find that it had been moved downhill about four inches. The silo leaned in the opposite direction, but on the whole, it was more upright. The siding had been pulled apart on the uphill side leaving three and four inch holes, and the roofing was in bad shape.

The trek to the orchard was dispiriting. Seventeen fruit-bearing trees had blown down, including mature apple trees and several cherry trees near the house. The elderberry patch up near the spring looked as if a steam roller had run over it. It was so flat it was almost unrecognizable.

The house itself showed only one major sign of a windstorm. The woodshed which was the last room on the L facing the hill had been broken into by the wind. The door had swung open and the door frame looked as if some giant had put his shoulder to it, lifting it up and spreading it out a couple of inches.

I walked down to the tenant house and found that the woodshed was awry and the roofing had mostly blown off. I saw that the north side of the house was now pocked marked as well, which meant it had taken quite a beating by hail as well as wind.

I walked back to our house and told Margret about all the damage to the property. She had made some breakfast and Barbara joined us, still half asleep, not knowing what all the excitement was about.

"What happened?" she asked as she yawned.

We just looked at each other and Margret said, "Not to worry."

"We're all okay and this all can be fixed." I said as I looked around the house.

In fact, it gave Margret a suggestion for a name for the farm.

"I think we should call this place "Windhill Farm."

"Well, maybe it should be "Windhill Farms, plural," I said, "since we have two houses and it's made up of eight parcels of land."

That made sense to Margret, and Windhill Farms became its official name.

Chapter 5
The Bees

The fall of 1940, Barbara started high school at Northeast Bradford High School in Rome, Pennsylvania, with intentions of going back to school in New York City later in the year. She rode the school bus from Windham Center and traveled about ten miles to and from school each day. But it seemed the methods of teaching were more practical in Rome than those used around New York and my daughter did so well that she didn't want to leave. Grace Huddle volunteered to let her board with them for the winter, so we let Barbara stay with the Huddles while we went back to the city. We figured it was better to stay in the city instead of dealing with the harsh winter months in our house in Pennsylvania. We lived in the studio apartment and I worked hard when there was work to do. We drove back to the farm for a couple of days every two or three weeks, weather permitting, to see Barbara and to take care of any needs of the farm.

During that winter when we were in New York, we received a telephone call from Grace Huddle. Barbara had fallen quite sick. Grace was nursing her, but felt that as her parents, we should know. Margret and I dropped everything to head for the

Huddle's farm. We arrived late that afternoon and were glad to see that Barbara was feeling better.

"Daddy, I was so sick, I could hardly breathe," my daughter said to us. "Aunt Grace put some sort of smelly gook on my chest. Oh, it smelled awful! I had to get well just so I wouldn't have to smell that stuff! I'm so glad you came. I missed you and I love you." She began to cry as we hugged our little girl.

We found out from Grace that it was a combination of cow paddy and spider webs to make some sort of poultice that drew out the infection.

"It works!" Grace said. "It might smell bad, but by God, it works!"

We were a little shocked by what Grace said she put on our daughter's chest, but she was right, it worked or maybe Barbara was right… she HAD to get better so she wouldn't have to smell that awful odor.

When Barbara was feeling better, we took her back to the city with us. Barbara, although not a Quaker, was entered at Friends Seminary. The school was walking distance from where our apartment was in the Gramercy Park area. She really liked it there and made many good friends. We were glad she was with us.

Come spring of 1941, we were again all set to go to the farm, but I had not been able to save enough money to keep us going for the entire summer. I had been worried about what to do when out of the blue a couple of artists (a man and his wife) heard about my ability to teach art and wrote to me about coming to the farm to study.

"Well, this is strange," I said as I read the letter. "They can't be serious. They would have to rough it while staying here since everything at the farm is so out of order. I was planning to paint the main house."

"Go ahead and respond," said Margret. "Let them know of your intentions to paint the house and that if they didn't mind you climbing up and down off of a step ladder to give them lessons that we wouldn't mind, either."

"I'll let them know that I don't really have a studio at the farm and no plans to put them up for the summer. If they could find a place to stay, I would be glad to teach them for six weeks," I decided.

I mailed a response letter and gave it no more thought. The following Thursday, we received a telegram informing us that they wished to drive over to the farm for an interview the following Monday. I suppose the whole idea sounded romantic to them over in Akron, Ohio, but I really didn't know what to make of the situation other than to prepare for visitors as best we could.

Monday morning came around and about ten o'clock, Barbara rushed in shouting, "I think they're here! There's a car pulling up in the driveway!"

The three of us went outside to greet the occupants of the car, and yes, they were the prospective students. The young lady was quite attractive with her long blonde hair and slim figure. Her husband, a nice looking man with dark hair and ocean blue eyes, stood by their car.

"Hello, we're the Tuckers," he said as he held out his hand to me. We shook hands and he continued, "My name is Joe and this is my wife Mary." She also held her hand out for a courtesy hand shake.

I introduced myself and my family, and told them to call me Van.

"This is a beautiful place," Mary said as she looked around. "It's so nice to be out here in the countryside."

"Come on inside," Margret said as she led the couple through the front door, Barbara and I following her. "We'll make some tea and take it out to sit under the maple tree. It's cooler there." Margret gathered all the tea things and put them on a tray.

"Yes, we have some things to discuss," I said as I carried the tray outside and placed it on a wooden picnic table in the shade. "Here, sit down and we'll figure out what we can do."

I motioned to the old metal lawn chairs next to the table. The artist couple sat down and put their tea cups on a small apple crate between the chairs.

"As I mentioned in my letter, we are really not ready to house anyone. As you can see the place needs a lot of work." I continued to explain, seating myself. "But if you can find somewhere to board for six weeks, I'll agree to teach you. Our tenant house is not in use and needs too much work for you to stay there, but it could work as a studio. There are broken out windows and the roof leaks a little."

"Is there anyone around that might put us up for six weeks?" Joe asked.

"I don't know," I replied, "but after you've finished your tea, we can get into your car and drive down to the gas station and see if they might know someone that you could board with."

When we were finished relaxing, Joe, Mary and I drove down to Allen's Filling Station and inquired if anyone around would take in a boarder for the summer. We learned from Allen of three possibilities. One of the three was Nellie Lawrence, whom we had met through the Huddles and lived about two miles down the road from us. We drove over to meet her and Nellie was delighted at the prospect of paying boarders for six weeks.

"Great!" Joe said. "Now we can plan our summer. We'll be back in a week."

They drove me back to the house and we let Margret know what the plan was. Joe, Mary and I chatted more about what I would teach them and how we could work out a schedule.

"Thank you so much," Joe said, when we had the schedule laid out. "It's going to be a wonderful summer."

"Oh yes," Mary excitedly said as she got into the car. "Can't wait to get started!"

Sure enough, in a week's time they returned and set up work in the tenant house. The lessons in drawing, painting, illustration and design started early in the morning, with Joe and Mary practicing on their own in the afternoon while I did my farm repairs. They were enthusiastic students and learned quickly.

It was about this same period that I was having a great time trying to get a colony of bees started, Floyd Williams having finally talked me into it. He had given me detailed instructions as to what to order from the bee supply company, which was good as I hadn't a clue as to all the things I would need. I ordered and received a beekeepers' outfit consisting of a helmet with a bee veil for self-protection, a smoke maker to calm the bees for inspection and honey gathering, a chisel-like affair for opening hives, the flattened hive box kits themselves, the frames for the insides, beeswax foundation for the bees to start working on, and a book called Beekeeping Simplified.

The bees were to be sent for after I had assembled and painted the hive boxes and put the frames together. I did this quite meticulously and was proud of the new home for the bees. When I was ready, I ordered a three-pound package of the recommended Italian bees, and when they arrived, I dumped them into the hive and placed the queen bee according to the directions. The queen bee came in a separate little box and had to be gotten out of her confinement within a few days by the bees eating away at one of the wax-like entrances. By the time they were done, she would smell like the rest of the bees and be accepted as their queen. I found it all interesting and took the top off of the hive every few days to see how my new bee family was coming along. They progressed according to the way Floyd said they should. Floyd came up several times the first couple of weeks to look at them and answer any of my questions.

Three weeks went by as usual when suddenly I went running in the house yelling excitedly, "The baby bees have hatched out!"

After I'd made a lot more fuss over them, Margret said as she was baking bread in the kitchen, "You act just like a new father."

It was not until then that I realized how exciting and interesting a colony of bees could be.

"This hatching out of new bees was what we've been waiting for," I explained. "It means that the colony is coming along all right and the older bees that are dying off are being replaced by many more young bees."

"It's a wonder they like you at all," Margret noted. "You take their house apart every day or two to study them."

"Guess we must have gotten acquainted," I replied proudly. "Even though I am quite a novice in the art of beekeeping, I never got a single sting."

One Sunday morning, Floyd drove up to the house and informed me that a farmer that lived nearby had several colonies of bees that he wanted to sell.

"I'm going up to his farm to buy his honey extractor and wanted to know if you would like to go along?" he asked.

"Sure!" I answered eagerly.

I grabbed my smoker and bee veil and got into Floyd's car. We drove about ten miles to the farm and Floyd bought the extractor as was pre-arranged. I asked about the bees, wanting to increase the size of my hives. After dickering for about an hour, the farmer agreed to sell me his five colonies of bees quite reasonably. There was only one thing left to do before completing the deal and that was to open the hives to see if there was any disease present. Floyd thought there might be something wrong when he noticed how some of the bees acted around the hives. He blew a few puffs of smoke in through the entrance and handed me the smoker, telling me to keep it going. But the smoke that we'd started with turned out to not be enough, because bees attacked us as soon as the lid was pried open.

"Oh NO! They're everywhere and not very happy!" I yelled, continuing to smoke them.

Floyd grabbed the smoker from me and laid a nice smoke screen over the top of the honey, which was built up most every-which-way in the box. We soon saw that the owner had known nothing about beekeeping. There were a couple of honey frames in the hive, but the bees had built honeycombs over and above them in odd and complex formations.

"I have never seen such a mess of bees before," I noted.

The bees were big black ones swarming around us. Floyd had handed me the smoker back, and I shot smoke at my wrists to protect them as the ordinary pig-skin dress glove slipped from under my sleeves. Thousands of bees filled the air as Floyd pried out a frame. In doing so he got stung a couple of times, but he brushed the stingers out like the veteran that he was. He took the frame aside and examined it for foul brood and unfortunately found many. The foul brood was an indication of disease. Floyd put the frame back and closed the hive.

"Sorry, no deal," he informed the disappointed farmer for me.

On our way home, Floyd asked, "Did you get stung, Van?"

"No," I answered.

"Well," Floyd said surprised "good! That might have ended your beekeeping. That was one of the worst messes of bees that I have ever seen and I wanted to see if you were afraid."

"I wasn't afraid, but I do realize the seriousness of some bee stings." I said. "Margret used to be afraid of bees. It seemed as though she would get stung if a bee sighted her. I remember two different occasions where bees had gotten into the car while driving and had stung her. At first she shied away from my bees, but before long she ignored them completely when they buzzed around the house or in the kitchen. She finally would show the stray bee out the kitchen door with all gentleness and even come out to look at the hive once in awhile.

Chapter 6
Chicago Here We Come

We had a grand and glorious time that summer of 1941, if you like working hard all the time. Margret and Barbara painted and wallpapered the inside of the house to their liking. I took on the task of painting the outside of the house. Painting was definitely needed, not only for improving the looks of the place, but for the protection of the wood. The house had not been painted for many years and it was difficult to get the remaining old paint off so that the new paint could go on. I tried the old stunt of burning it off with a blow torch, but only succeeded in burning the wood. There was no oil left in the paint to bubble up and be scraped off. After trying many methods, I discovered that scraping it vigorously with a flat plasterer trowel proved the easiest and most efficient. This job took several weeks in and of itself, while I fiddled around with many little jobs as well as devoting some time to teaching.

After the thorough scraping, I tried spraying the house with a paint sprayer that could be attached to the motor of the car for air pressure. In this attempt, I spotted my nice green car and my daughter's bicycle with white house paint! Many mixtures of paint were tried, but none of them seemed to cover satisfactorily, so I set out to paint by brush. The result was much better, but the first coat soaked into the dry wood, requiring three times the amount specified by the paint manufacturer for the first layer. After it had dried properly, the second coat of paint went on quite easily. The final result astonished us all -- the old house became beautiful! The Tuckers came up to admire the paint job that had been done.

I looked at the contrast between the house and the dilapidated front porch and I finally said, "It's become obvious that the front porch needs to come off."

"Need some help?" Joe asked.

"Sure, let's get started," I said.

I rounded up some tools and handed Joe a crowbar. We started yanking the porch off then and there. It took most of the afternoon because we had to remove above and around the porch as well. The process required some intricate patching with lumber taken from the side of the tenant house, since no standard lumber was of that width and thickness.

After finishing the outside paint job, I took photographs which showed that we'd enhanced the exterior by a hundredfold.

"It really looks so much better," I remarked to Joe, satisfied. "Thanks for helping out."

That summer we had callers almost every evening or went out somewhere and we took the Tuckers with us. Joe and Mary proved to be pleasant company as well as good students. We drove about forty miles to Binghamton, New York, to see movies and eat steak suppers. Throughout the summer we attended nearby town festivals in Nichols and Windham Center. Many suppers were held in connection with several of the town's churches. About one evening a week, Joe and I joined in a little game of poker with the village doctor, postmaster and several prominent businessmen of the community.

Sue Benson, a wonderful woman living on the opposite side of Nichols, would barbecue chicken every Wednesday evening when weather permitted. She had a beautiful log cabin situated along the Wappasening Creek. The pines surrounding her place gave it a quiet beauty. We always looked forward to being called and told what dish to bring to Sue's for Wednesday night supper. Four or five families bringing a large dish, a cake or pie, and all "chipping in twenty-five cents" towards the chicken; she gave us quite a feast. We were able to get acquainted with people that it might have otherwise taken years to meet.

At the end of the six weeks, it was time for the Tuckers to go back to Ohio.

"You two have been such good students and good friends as well. We hate to see you leave," I said as I helped them with their suitcases.

"We had a wonderful time here and learned so much from you, Van," Joe said. "You taught us more than just how to paint and draw, you also taught us how to respect nature."

"I enjoyed getting to know you and your lovely family," Mary said as she shook my hand. "You take care Margret and you too, Barbara," as she hugged Margret and Barbara. "We'll keep in touch."

As a result of this experience, Joe and Mary had become country conscious and vowed that they should return again sometime to rusticate.

Labor Day came, and for many years a homecoming was held in Nichols, New York. People living miles away poured into town to see a parade in the morning, a baseball game in the afternoon, and have both lunch and supper at the town park. In the evening, there was square dancing in which both young and old participated on even terms. Labor Day was bittersweet, because after Labor Day we returned to New York City for the winter. One good thing was that Barbara was glad to see her friends at Friends Seminary School.

My work was slow and many artists were sitting around in studios doing nothing. I was getting concerned living in New York City about when and where I might see my next paycheck.

"You know, things are getting bad in Europe," said John, one of my artist friends. "Not sure what might happen next as to whether the USA will get into this war."

"I agree," I said. "Things in general seem to be unsettled. I've got a family to support and maybe my freelancing isn't going to work out. I need to think about getting a full time paying job."

That evening, Margret and I did some serious talking about what we should do.

Margret suggested, "Why don't the three of us drive to the farm for the weekend to think things over."

"That sounds like a good idea," I said as I reached for the phone. "But, let me call some art directors and ask if they know of any good job openings. I have got to earn some money."

It felt good to be at the farm again and to get away from the noise of the city. As we sat outside looking at the sun going down behind the mountain, Margret almost reluctantly said, "Van, I hate to burden you with one more thing to worry about, but…"

"What's wrong?" I said as I reached for her hand.

"I wasn't sure, but now..." she hesitated for a moment, "I'm pregnant."

"What, after all these years?" I turned and faced her and smiled and put my arms around her to comfort her. "It's okay, I mean, I think it's wonderful! I love you and we'll make it work, you'll see."

We hugged and she cried in relief. She stood up and walked towards the kitchen to retrieve a tissue to wipe her eyes.

When she came back, Margret said, "I was so worried you would be upset, especially now with the way things are going with work and maybe a war. I just didn't think it was the best time to be pregnant. I mean, I never would have thought after all this time that I would get pregnant again."

"Don't worry, things will work out for us; they always do," I said reassuringly.

Barbara came outside just then, so Margret told her, "You're going to have a brother or sister."

"What!" Barbara yelped. "You're pregnant? Mom! Are you serious...really? I can't believe it!"

Margret was relieved that Barbara was going to be okay with the situation and Barbara was excited that she would have a baby brother or sister. We discussed, as a family, the possibilities of what we might need to do. We were torn about staying in the city or maybe moving back to the farm full time, but then what?

When we arrived back in the city on Monday morning, we still weren't sure what to do. While we were still talking about the pregnancy, the telephone rang about eleven that morning. It was a long distance call from Chicago.

"Hello, this is Marshall Field from Chicago," the man said on the phone. "We're starting a new newspaper in Chicago to compete with the Chicago Daily Tribune. I understand you are looking for a job and wanted to know if you could come to Chicago and organize the map department. I understand that you used to draw maps when you worked for the Associated Press."

"Why yes, I did draw maps and yes, I might be interested," I said as I looked at Margret who was listening. "When did you want me there?"

"As soon as possible," he answered. "We would like to get the Chicago Sun up and running before the end of this year."

"Well," I paused. "I need to make some arrangements here and pack up and ship items to some place there. We will need to find a place to live!"

"We can set you up in a furnished house," he suggested. "I'll even pay for the first month's rent. How soon can you get here?"

"We can be there on Saturday," I said and hoped I could get everything ready by then.

"Great! I'll mail you an advance check and an address where you will be living and of course where to come to work on Monday morning."

The offer of an instant job, with an instant paycheck, trumped everything else for the moment. We started packing the studio at once, deciding what would go to Chicago and what would go to the farm. Wednesday, we drove back to the farm and made arrangements for a moving van to haul our belongings and equipment from the studio to the farm and we closed out the studio apartment in New York. We made sure that the Huddles would give the moving people access to the house to store our New York belongings in the large parlor room, since we would not be there to oversee it ourselves. We then went around saying our "good-byes" to our friends and neighbors and to our wonderful little farmhouse.

Charlie Barlow, our handyman, said he would jack up our car and store it in the horse barn. We were grateful to them all, and thanked them for what they would do for us. The Huddles drove us to Waverly to catch the overnight train to Chicago on Friday afternoon and we arrived in Chicago early Saturday morning.

My family and I took a cab to the address I'd been given on West Grace Street where we would

 be living. It was a family-type neighborhood with bungalow houses on both sides of the street and the Irving Park Elementary School right across the street. We could see children playing outside and people sitting on their porches. Our house, too, was a small bungalow with wood-lap siding painted tan with dark green trim and shutters and a small porch. We unlocked the door with the key that had been mailed to us, and walked inside to see a fully furnished home, including dishes, pots and pans, towels, and bedding. The house had three small bedrooms, one bath, living room, a small kitchen and a screened in back porch overlooking a small fenced yard.

"I want this bedroom," Barbara announced after poking about the place. "I like looking out this window and seeing the yard out back. Someone has planted flowers and there's a nice big oak tree that we could sit under in the afternoon."

The room she'd chosen had a single bed with a quilt on it, and next to the bed was a night stand with a small lamp, a dresser on the opposite wall and a small stuffed chair next to the window.

"It's cozy in here, isn't it?" Barbara said as she sat on the bed, bouncing up and down to check the mattress.

Margret checked out what would be our bedroom that faced the front of the house. It was across the hall from the other two bedrooms. The room was larger and had a double bed, dresser, and a pair of night stands with lamps on each flanking the bed. The third bedroom, also on the back side of the house, was much smaller and probably would be good for storage for a while or maybe the baby's room. It was nice that all we had to bring was our clothes and personal items.

"Actually," Margret said with a smile, "this house is quite nice." She checked the closet space and inspected the small bathroom, which was next to the larger bedroom. "Oh look, it has one of those wonderful claw foot tubs. I'll enjoy that tub."

The kitchen had a gas stove, refrigerator and enough room for a small kitchen table and four chairs. There were not many cabinets, but it did have a small pantry.

"I like how they decorated everything," Barbara noted as she glanced into the living room with its sofa, coffee table and a big stuffed chair. "Look, even a bookcase!"

Though we missed Windhill Farms, we nevertheless spent the day unpacking our suitcases and boxes to make the house our home for this next part of the journey of our lives.

Chapter 7
The War Years

Margret, Barbara and I settled in our little bungalow house and I started working at the Chicago Sun Newspaper. It took some time to hire people to run a new newspaper. I set up what would be the Map Department. I would be Art Director for this department and would be working on maps for the paper showing the latest areas of Europe and other countries that are involved in the War. I had no idea how involved I would need to be as the war continued on.

On December 7th, 1941, the newspaper printed out a large headline "JAPANESE BOMBED PEARL HARBOR!" My co-workers and I listened to President Roosevelt on the radio as he announced the US was entering the war. We were concerned about what might happen next. I heard of many young men joining the military as a result of Pearl Harbor and the President's speeches, but I was in my late thirties and probably too old to be thinking about being in the military, not to mention I had a family with a baby on the way.

After that headliner day, I was kept busy day and night for many weeks. I learned a lot about map drawing while I had worked at the

Associated Press years ago and now was drawing maps of certain areas where the Germans were heading in Europe. Listening to the radio and reading the news of the war in Europe, I was able to produce many of the maps ahead of time. I would study how the enemy was traveling across Europe and I could tell where the next combat zone would be. I would draw the maps up ahead of time, so that when the battles were fought, I would have the maps ready for print. My zeal for the paper got me into a little hot water, though. One day my boss called me into his office, a grave tone in his voice.

"Van," said Mr. Kolliker, "there are some government officials here to talk to you." He introduced a heavy set man as Agent Stone and another man that was just the opposite with his thin framed body as Agent Hadley.

I asked, "Can I help you?"

"Yes," said Agent Stone, holding up his identification badge from the Office of Strategic Services.

"We've noticed that when the paper comes out, the maps show exactly where the enemy was and well, we want to know how or where you are getting that information. How would you know where the next battle would be the day before it happens?"

He slammed a newspaper down on the desk and pointed at one of my maps printed a couple of days previously.

"Yeah, how could you know ahead of time before the incidents happen?" Agent Hadley demanded.

"Oh, well that's easy," I said as I pulled out some other maps. "If you will just follow the path the enemy is taking, you can easily figure out where their next move would be."

I pointed out which way the enemy was headed and also told them where I thought they would go next. They studied the map and finally agreed that it could happen that way. After the discussion, the two agents headed out the door and I could hear Agent Stone say, "Maybe Mr. Van Swearingen needs to show his maps to the military." I just chuckled to myself.

In February of 1942, I went over to The Chicago Tribune to look over the competition. I liked their setup and also met a nice group of people there. A few weeks passed and I was pleasantly surprised to be offered a higher-paying job at "The Trib" doing more than just drawing maps everyday – they would also give me other assignments where they needed sketches. I felt a little guilty about leaving the Chicago Sun, but I had to think of caring for my family. I gave my notice to 'The Sun', and on April 1st, 1942, I started working at the Chicago Tribune.

During the war months, as we came to call them later, Margret of course, was growing closer to her due date. She complained a lot and hated being pregnant. While I was getting ready for work, I heard Margret cry out in pain from the bedroom.

"Van!" Margret yelled out. "It's time!"

"Oh my God, are you sure?" I asked as I ran to her and watched her hold her stomach and yell out in pain and noticed water on the floor.

"YES, I'm sure!" she said, panting. "MY WATER JUST BROKE!"

"Barbara!" I yelled out. "Your mother is going to have a baby, NOW!" Barbara grabbed the overnight suitcase she had packed days earlier, while I called a cab. When the car arrived I helped Margret get into the cab and off we went to Saint Hospital, which was only five miles away. "Hurry, hurry," my wife cried out!

After waiting and pacing in the hallway on Monday, May 25th, 1942, a nurse finally came out to let me and Barbara know that my wife was fine and I had a healthy baby boy.

"Oh, Daddy!" Barbara yelled as she hugged me. "She did it! I have a baby brother!"

We went into her room and I saw my son for the first time. He had a full head of dark hair. I leaned over to Margret and gave her a kiss on her forehead and said, "I love you and I'm so glad you're okay."

"Look at that hair," Barbara noted as she softly patted his head.

"You were born with a head full of hair, too," Margret said. "And you still have thick long dark hair." Margret repositioned herself in bed. "Here, Van, you hold your son," as she slowly handed me this tiny little bundle.

"We have a son," I said softly as I held him in my arms for the first time. "Welcome to our family."

We named him Earl Cornelius Van Swearingen, Jr., but we nicknamed him Neil from his middle name Cornelius. When we brought little Neil home, Barbara, who was now fifteen, helped Margret take care of him. She enjoyed having a little brother and loved to take him out in the stroller to show him off in the nearby park. Barbara got a chuckle when some people thought she was the mother, though I was less amused.

Barbara had done so well at Friends Seminary in NYC that she was able to skip a grade at Carl Schurz High School in Chicago and graduated that June of 1942. We were so proud of her.

I worked hard that summer at the paper, but we never forgot about the farm. I made some time to study Farm Management from one of the State Colleges through their extension department. This was my third farm course. I had learned what not to invest in and some of the many pitfalls. I enjoyed all the courses. I also collected

Farmers Bulletins from the Department of Agriculture in Washington, DC, on many subjects pertaining to farms, as well as some bulletins from the State College. Most state colleges furnish bulletins on practically any problem that might confront a farmer. Efficiency methods are given special attention, and I took full advantage of them. Farm magazines proved to be a great source of inspiration, and so I subscribed to The Rural New Yorker, The Pennsylvania Farmer and The Country Gentleman. A plan began to form about what I wanted to do with the farm and Margret gave me wholehearted approval.

The fall of 1942, I finally got a week's vacation and decided to check on the farm. Traveling was being discouraged because of the war, so I left my family in Chicago while I took the train to Waverly and had Ned Huddle greet me at the station.

"Ah, it's good to be back," I said as I got out of his truck and stood there looking at our farmhouse.

"It's good to have ya back. We've been keepin' an eye out and I think things are just the way ya left 'em," Ned said. "Let me know if ya need anything," he added as he backed his truck down the driveway to return to his own farm.

It was nice to be "home" again. I walked out back to check on the colony of bees, and was glad to see they were quite active for that time of year.

They had made enough honey to support themselves for the winter, which was all that could have been expected, since they'd had no particular care. I made a mental note to make arrangements with Floyd Williams to take the colony down to his apiary and care for them properly before I left again.

Since gasoline was rationed and my car was still up on blocks in the horse barn, I took Barbara's bicycle and visited several of the neighbors to get reacquainted. The Huddles had me come down each evening for supper, which was a treat, since I didn't do much cooking.

Each day, I kept busy straightening out odds and ends that we had left undone before moving to Chicago. I cleaned out closets, swept the whole house, put away the cord of wood and straightened up the furniture that had been brought by the movers from our old New York apartment. I pruned the apple trees that Ned planted the previous year to take the place of those blown down by the big storm.

A couple of the evenings, I was invited to Doc Brown's for a poker game and Dave, the town's postman, invited me for supper one evening. I was glad to have so many friends to see while I was there alone.

The last day, Dave drove me to the railway station in Waverly for my trip back to Chicago. During the long train ride, I thought about all the friends we had made in that farming community. Chicago was nothing like that. We barely knew our neighbors on our street. People in the city just kept to themselves. The train pulled into the station in Chicago and Margret greeted me with a hug and kiss. It was good to be back with my family. That evening over supper, I told them about how the farm was and what was going on with our friends.

After a few weeks, I noticed that there was a little tension between Barbara and my wife. I wasn't sure what was going on. Neil was a handful, and maybe that was it. He did cry a lot and at times would get angry and bang his head on the wall. Barbara helped Margret take care of Neil and as he started to talk, he called her "Big Sis." I could tell that even my daughter was having problems with controlling Neil.

Barbara approached me after Margret had left to run some errands.

"Daddy," Barbara said clearing her throat. "Mom seems to always find something else to do or somewhere to go. I feel like I'm raising YOUR son."

"Now, Barbara," I interrupted. "I'm sorry you feel like that, but she needs your help. I'm sure she just thinks you are doing so well with Neil and he loves you so much."

"I know, and I'll try harder to be more patient," she quietly acknowledged. "I just don't know if I can keep on taking care of him with his crying and temper tantrums. He's too much for me to handle sometimes."

"Do you want me to speak to your mother?" I asked.

"I don't know," Barbara said as she held her head down, trying to hold back the tears.

"Come on," I said as I was trying to cheer her up. "Let's see if any of that cake is left in the kitchen."

The next vacation I was able to get from the newspaper came the first two weeks in September of 1943, and we decided we wanted to go back to Windhill Farms. Surprisingly, the weather was good and the trains weren't crowded as we traveled. It was unusual, because the war had really gotten under way and soldiers were riding the trains to their postings.

The train arrived in Waverly on a Saturday night. It was eleven o'clock and we had made arrangements with Doc Brown to buy us groceries and other supplies, meet us at the train station, and drive us out to the farm. However, the Doctor's wife made other plans, and had arranged that we stay with them that night. We enjoyed the evening and the following morning the Browns gave us a big breakfast. We all talked over old times and told them about Chicago. We had so much to talk about, it was noon before Doc Brown could drive us to the farm.

Margret and Barbara were excited to get back home. And, although it was the first time our two-year-old son Neil was there, he walked around as if he'd always lived at Windhill Farms. My wife and daughter started working on making the house cozy again. Electricity had been brought over the hill to the farm while we were gone and it was quite an experience for Margret to turn on the fluorescent lights that Ned had installed for us in the kitchen and to start the electric refrigerator. But, best of all, as far as I was concerned, we could finally use our electric toaster. We appreciated Ned watching over our house while we were gone.

The hills were so beautiful that time of year that we sat and talked after lunch and admired the scenery out the living room window. The bay window faced southwest and let in a portion of the fall sunlight.

"Let's walk down to the tenant house," Margret suggested as she cleared the dishes off the table. "I would like to see how it looks now that Floyd has put on the roof and painted the house."

"I'm glad we hired him to do the work," I said. "It's nice not having to do it myself."

"Come on Neil, let's go for a walk," as I placed Neil on my shoulders. "You get to see the rest of Windhill Farms."

As we walked, we could see rabbits hopping along the road. They didn't even seem to be afraid of us. We had to shoo them out of the way. Neil laughed at them and wanted me to pick up a rabbit for him to carry.

"Oh no, we're not going to have a pet rabbit," I informed him.

When we got to the tenant house, we found that the weeds had grown up waist high in the yard, and that a mass of burr bushes seemed to have sprung up around the door. By carefully placing an extended foot on the bottom of a burr bush, I found that I could push it down and make a path without getting burrs all over my pant legs.

The old pad lock was rusty, but unlocked with ease. Although the outside of the house looked beautiful, the inside was a mess. Plaster was partially off most of the walls, leaving large gaping spaces where the wall boards showed through. The floor boards were uneven and warped, probably because water had dripped through the roof before it had been replaced.

Margret dashed from room to room and finally exclaimed, "Let's finish fixing up this house! The view from the window is so beautiful. Look, you can see Mina Allen's place and Windham Center from this window."

I put Neil down on the floor and he immediately tried to eat a piece of plaster.

"Barbara, get that away from your brother!" Margret said as she pointed to Neil, "Keep an eye on him and make sure he doesn't get into anything else."

Barbara picked Neil up and carried him upstairs to check the bedrooms up. We followed, wanting to see if the damage was as extensive as on the first floor.

"I'd take this bedroom if we were going to live here!" she said as she put Neil back down on the floor and looked around the upstairs area.

"Well, if we could find someone to take care of any future livestock, he would have to live at the main house since that's where the barns and fenced pastures are," I pondered. "We could stay in the tenant house when we visited."

"How about asking Charlie Barlow?" Margret suggested. "Charlie would know how to do all that."

As we walked back to the main house we stopped to pick some apples, filling our pockets and arms for later eating. When we arrived back at the house, Margret and Barbara continued organizing while I spent the remainder of the day fixing the refrigerator door, which didn't close properly, and getting the hand pump for the well to operate. The leather washer in the pump had dried out, and fortunately only needed a soaking and spreading at the outer rim.

Over supper we talked merrily about our plans and what we hoped would happen for Windhill Farms' future.

Chapter 8
Dreams and Plans

A couple of days later, Margret, Barbara and I decided to spend a few minutes with the Huddles. Grace asked lots of questions about Chicago.

Margret answered her, "To be honest, we're not that crazy about Chicago. I would rather live here in the country. It's too busy, noisy and dirty!"

Ned talked about his large herd of Holstein cows, the barns, his new milking machines and milk cooler. I was glad, because that was a great lead-in to what I wanted to ask him.

I leaned over to Ned and Donald and said, "My wife and I want your opinion on having someone live at our farm to take care of things. They could manage a herd of cows. With the war going into its second year, it seems a shame not to have our farm producing something."

"I know someone who might be interested in takin' care of yur place," Donald said. "He works on a farm about fifteen miles from here in Le Rampville, but would like to move back up this way. Ya might know his brother, Bill Harding."

That sounded interesting – I thought it would be good to have someone with whom we had a connection, however slight, to live at Windhill Farms. Before the evening closed, Donald said that he could write Ted Harding in the morning to ask him to come and see me.

The next morning was Labor Day, which meant it was the highlight of Old Home Week Festival in Nichols. This small town was only about five miles from where we lived, but it was actually in New York and not Pennsylvania, still we felt like it was our hometown anyway. We made a special effort to be there, because we knew that we would meet some of our old friends. Doc Brown came up at nine-thirty and drove us down to his house, which was located in downtown Nichols. It was a fresh and invigorating morning, weather-wise, and there was a lot of action in the neighborhood and in their home.

Barbara, Neil, Doc Brown, and I sat on the porch waiting for the parade to come along, while Margret was helping Mrs. Brown with food preparations. A blare of music from the town band announced its beginning and two horses, one white and one black, completely out of step with each other, came around the corner up Main Street. These were followed by cowboys from a rodeo outfit that had been hired for the day. Most of these cowboys looked like old men 4F's rejected from the Army. Several floats came by next representing the Red Cross workers, the Good Farmer, the Country Doctor with his old horse and buggy, a couple of clowns and a little Queen of something or other. Following the floats was an old dilapidated wagon full of children of all ages. The children belonged to the driver. Several more cowboys and wagons with village trade and merchant ads appeared and the procession was trailed by several automobiles and an old stagecoach. Women and children dressed in costumes from the eighteen hundreds, sat erect inside the coach, waving to the small groups here and there on the street.

The little town of Nichols wholeheartedly participated in the parade leaving few to watch it. Neil waved at the people going by and laughed at the clowns. The parade was headed for the town park. I borrowed Doc's car and drove Mrs. Brown and the ham to the picnic area. The doctor was busy with a patient in his office. I brought the car back and Margret, Barbara, Neil and I meandered over to the park. We stopped and talked with many friends on the way. By the time we arrived, there was a long line waiting for tickets and plates for the dinner. We finally were able to get tickets and sat at a picnic table. Dinner was ham, green beans, pinto beans, biscuits, potato salad and chocolate cake for dessert. All contributed by neighbors.

After dinner the four of us browsed around the park, speaking with old friends. Barbara finally broke away from us, leaving Neil with Margret, and went with her girlfriends. She had not seen them for quite a while and had a lot of catching up to do.

We had just found seats to watch the ball game, when Neil got so sleepy that it was really a shame to keep him awake. Margret wanted to take him home, so I borrowed Doc's car and took them back to the farm. I returned the car and walked back to the park and spotted Barbara with her friends.

Old Dick, who stayed with the Huddles, was there in his "Sunday-go-to meetin" clothes and hailed me for a long talk. Dick was generally quiet except on the occasions where he imbibed a bit. After his third or fourth drink, Dick usually was no longer seventy-three in his mind, he wasn't even over thirty. His silence would drop and he would become quite garrulous as everyone became his closest friend.

We walked into the grandstand to watch the baseball game where I spotted Charlie Barlow. Dick drifted away as the game came to a close. Barlow offered Barbara and me a ride back to the farm. We stopped by the Doc's house to let him know we had a ride and thanked him for such a nice day.

"You know, I can easily get your car running if you wanted to drive it back to Chicago," Charlie said conversationally on the ride back home.

"I'll need a new license plate for it, but sure, if you can get it running again, that would be great," I said. "I'll try and get one on Tuesday."

I had Charlie stop at the little house since I wanted to talk to him about my ideas for fixing it up. We spent an hour discussing what could be done to improve it.

I happened to have a sketch with me in my pocket and proceeded to show it to Charlie. Pointing to it, I explained, "Here is the plan which includes: tearing down the old central chimney which extends from the second floor and putting in a new foundation for the cellar and the fireplace in the living room. I also want a wall knocked out between the living room and the small bedroom next to it, to make a 13 x 22 foot living room."

"I'm really getting excited about this, Van," Charlie said. "This can really be a cute little house for you."

"Oh and here," I continued. "The stairwell in the kitchen needs to be moved to the center of the house. That way we could access each of the three bedrooms without walking through two bedrooms to get to the third one," I explained.

"What about the kitchen?" Charlie asked.

"The kitchen is 13 x 22 and can stay as it is, using the space as both kitchen and dining room. Oh, and one of the walls upstairs needs to be moved to the center of the house, making the two smaller bedrooms the same size, 11 x 13 each. The bedroom over the kitchen would be much larger, but I have trouble visualizing it because the stairwell is being moved to the opposite side and enclosed."

"Most of the door frames are crooked," Charlie noticed as we walked around the house inspecting the place. "I can straighten them and I can cover the walls with sheet rock instead of plaster."

"I would love to have the floors redone in oak, which will have to be sanded and stained and polished," I suggested. "It does seem like a lot to get accomplished."

"Guess it will keep me out of trouble for a while," Charlie said with a little chuckle as we got back into his car and he dropped us off at the main house.

The next day was Tuesday and Charlie came back at nine to put the wheels back on my car, install a new battery and get the car running. Later that afternoon, I attached the new license tag to the car and washed it so it didn't look so shabby. Since the car was out of the barn, I decided to spend a couple of days cleaning the old horse barn out. Manure was stuck to the floor in some places in huge chunks. When the previous tenant had left he hadn't bothered to clean it and this was my first attempt at "mucking." Before I finished the job, I regretted having ever started it, but the results were worthwhile.

A few days later, I drove the newly fixed car over to Floyd William's place. Floyd showed me two colonies of the bees that he was keeping for me. He then pulled out some filled jars of honey and insisted that I take them with me when I went back to Chicago.

"I didn't come here to get honey from you, but these twelve jars will come in handy since sugar is rationed," I said as I placed the honey in my car. "Thanks."

Over the next few weeks, we enjoyed visits with our neighbors. We spent several evenings with the Huddles. We enjoyed Grace's raspberries that she'd picked and preserved. The Franklins, from further down the road, came up to visit one afternoon and then invited us back to their house for supper that evening. Charlie Barlow came up one evening with his wife and family. He and I made more plans for the little house and I gave Charlie sketches of how we wanted the fireplace to look and government bulletins on how it should be constructed. The Barlows, the following night, had us down to their house for a delicious rabbit dinner. The rabbit was cooked so well that it was almost impossible to tell it from good chicken.

One afternoon, I had just gotten back from the old orchard, which was full of ripe apples, to find that Donald Huddle had arrived with Ted Harding, the fellow who wanted to work on the farm. I proposed buying eight cows in the spring and two or three or more cows in the Fall, also buying a team of horses before Fall, and that Ted and his family would take over the main house the following spring on April 1, 1944. Ted was agreeable, and although Ted's wife was not there, Ted and I shook hands on the deal. Ted and Donald left together around milking time, but in the meantime Doc, the Franklins and the Barlows drove up for a visit and stayed until after dark.

The next morning, I drove to Oswego, New York, to the rationing board to get ration coupons for gasoline so that we could drive the car back to Chicago. During the afternoon, Margret, Barbara, Neil, and I visited the newly planted orchard to replace the ones that got torn up in the windstorm that had given the farm its name. My son always was thrilled to ride on my shoulders, his black hair waving in the wind as he bounced around and laughed as if each time were a new adventure. It was the new orchard's second or third summer, but we were disappointed that the trees hadn't grown more. Most of them didn't look much bigger then they did at the end of the first year, but I supposed they were doing as well as they could with absolutely no care or tillage. From there we went up past the springs to the old orchard and sat eating apples.

Neil was becoming quite an "apple eater," so we had to discourage him from eating too many.

That evening, we read up on how to make grape jelly and the following morning, picked a couple of wash tubs of Concord grapes by the old dilapidated milk shed. I spoiled the first tub of grapes by cooking them too long. The juice tasted scorched, so there was nothing else to do but to dump it out. The second batch was excellent, since Margret had been in charge of cooking them. Before I had finished, grape juice had gotten most everywhere in the kitchen. I got reprimanded plenty for it by Margret, but couldn't seem to do much about it because my hands were dyed completely purple. We had plenty of grape jelly to take back to Chicago.

Ted drove up with his wife and family, unexpectedly. They had two boys, two and five year olds, and a daughter only a few months old. After looking over the buildings, Margret served tea and we talked about farming. Ted's wife had lived ten years of her life in our farmhouse several years before we had bought the farm and they both wanted to get back to Nichols. They said they would be happy to manage the farm.

As all good things must end, we had spent the last two days cleaning up the house and preparing to drive our car back to Chicago.

"Come on Barbara," Margret yelled out, "get your suitcase and books and put them in the car."

"I'm coming!" Barbara yelled back. "I can't find my jacket."

"Here it is," I responded as I found her jacket on the back of the kitchen chair. "I hope we got everything we need," as I looked around the house one more time and then closed the door.

We left Windhill Farms early on Friday morning. The fog had not completely lifted, but it was clear enough to drive. It was magical seeing the low clouds hanging on the mountain tops and rolling fog moving along the valley's rivers.

Barbara announced, "I'm calling the fog in the valley, Dragon's Breath."

"Oh, that's a cute name," Margret replied. "It does sort of remind me of what a dragon's breath might look like," and giggled. She then noticed something moving across the road.

"Oh look! Deer crossing up ahead! Slow down, Van."

"My goodness, it looks like a herd of deer," I said as I slowed down to a stop and we watched the deer crossing the road.

The next few years, we continued driving back and forth from the farm to Chicago. Each trip would bring us something new to marvel at or a new restaurant to stop and have lunch in some little town on the way. We tried to get out to the farm on long weekends or a couple of weeks' vacation during the summer months.

Charlie Barlow, with the help of Jim and Martha Greene, kept the wells clean. Water was pumped from the springs to the barn and house. We arranged, from afar, to have inside plumbing and finally a bathroom in the main house and the little house. Electricity was finally hooked up to the little house for a modern kitchen and an electric stove and refrigerator. Charlie Barlow, who worked on remodeling the little house, built us a beautiful wood burning fireplace. He put in oak floors and made it into a cozy place to live. On our quick trips back, Margret and I painted and fixed the inside of the little house. It became a charming, comfortable summer home. We loved walking in our fields and woods and going swimming at the nearby Wappasening Creek below our lower field.

Overall, Windhill Farms with its two houses, barns, orchards and added rose gardens, was a wonderful place to live. Margret loved to entertain and in return was invited to many homes of friends. The farm was the true answer to our dreams of a perfect summer home.

I had convinced Margret on the idea of making the farm into a dairy farm. We loved the idea that we would have a dairy farm to visit occasionally and see the new born calves added to the herd. I had investigated and learned that Holstein cows were the best milk producers. On our visits to the farm, we enjoyed seeing the black and white cows grazing in our pasture and were glad that our farm was being used as a farm. Hay was stored in the barn, a vegetable garden planted. Acres of wheat in one field and corn in another, it seemed perfect!

Unfortunately, it took almost three years and an honest feed store owner to let me in on the fact that Ted Harding was "stealing me blind."

"I thought you should know, that Ted hasn't been paying the feed bills," John, the feed store owner informed me.

"I had no idea this was happening and why I wasn't I told sooner?" I asked. I was angry that someone would do this. "I'll try and repay you as soon as I can. I might need to sell my herd of cows."

"I'm sorry, but as you know, I have a business to run," John replied.

I drove over to the Huddles to see what they might know about Ted.

"We had no idea that had been goin' on," Ned said, scratching his head. "We would see him time to time, but he really never said much to us."

I was still upset and drove down to approach Ted about the situation. He was sitting outside on the side porch when I pulled up the driveway.

"Ted," I said as I got out of the car, "We need to talk!" I tried to keep calm, but I think he knew I was upset and why.

"Ahh… how ya doing?" Ted hesitantly said as he stood up from his chair.

"Not so good!" I replied. "Why didn't you pay the feed bills with the money I sent to you? Where did that money go?

"I'm sorry, Mr. Van," he said. "I guess it just got outta hand. I lost my job in town and well, I had to feed my family, so we were livin' off of what you sent for the feed store."

"Why didn't you let me know? I could have made some sort of arrangement. I feel as though you stole from me, you deceived me and you lied!"

"You're right, I shouldn't have let it get that way," he apologized.

His wife and children were standing in the doorway and that didn't make it any easier for me to tell him, "You and your family are out of here! Get your stuff and move out!"

I drove back to the little house and told Margret what had happened. We both felt terrible about the situation and even worse that our dream farm was so misused.

After a few days, I had to call the Sheriff's department and legally had the Hardings evicted. The worst part was my having to auction off all of the cattle and barn equipment to pay the bills left by Ted. I hated having to sell all our purebred Holstein cows. I thought those cows were our future.

Chapter 9

Time For Changes

We did not regret buying the farm and loved our time there, but it was time to settle down where we belonged, especially since Margret was pregnant again. We decided to leave both the farm and Chicago. Windhill Farms would continue to be our part-time place, but we needed to be somewhere more stable – which to us meant moving back to Rye, New York. I continued to freelance and was able to keep a steady income doing magazine illustrations. We rented a small house on Ridgeland Terrace, while we were hoping to find a house to buy.

During her pregnancy, my wife would walk around the house complaining and saying she was so uncomfortable with her back hurting, her ankles swollen, and of course looking like a blimp in her eyes. During one of these reoccurring rants close to her due date, I tried to reason with her.

"I really didn't want another baby," Margret moaned as she stared at her stomach. "I'm forty years old, why would I want another child?"

"Now Margret," I replied. "You're beautiful and you're a wonderful mother and I love you."

"When this baby is born, YOU can take care of this child!" she cried.

"Your hormones are just getting the better of you," I said. "Now, just calm down."

"I'm so tired that I can't imagine taking care of another child!" she cried even harder.

"You'll feel differently when you finally get to hold our new baby." I tried to sooth her.

"Oh sure, and then I get to feed the baby in the middle of the night while you're sleeping. I'm the one who has to feed it and change the diapers and put up with the crying! I am really NOT looking forward to raising another child!"

The best thing I thought I could do was to just keep my mouth shut. I thought I had said enough, and I was glad that Barbara hadn't witnessed this particular conversation. Margret finally calmed down and the next thing was her fixing up the future baby's room with cute little stuffed animals.

A few more weeks went by and Margret was ready to have that baby, she was complaining all the time. Finally, the morning of May 16, 1945 we rushed to United Hospital and my wife gave birth at 10:10 a.m.

"Van," said Margret frantically. "The newborn has some complications with her not being able to intake milk! The doctor wants to keep her here for awhile to see if she improves."

After a week in the hospital, the problem with her intestine was resolved and she was able to come home. We called the baby Phyllis and

Margret introduced Neil to his little sister. He looked at her and touched her head lightly. Neil had always called Barbara Big Sis and now he had a Little Sis. "She's so tiny," Neil said as he stared at his new little sister. Margret was depressed for a while after the birth and Barbara ended up taking care of both Neil and the newborn.

Watching Barbara stomp into the room, I could tell she was upset and was trying to hold back tears. I hadn't realized how the new baby was affecting her.

"Mom," Barbara said, pacing back and forth, "I'm afraid of taking care of Phyllis. I'm worried she'll die on me."

"Oh Barbara, don't be so dramatic, she's fine," Margret said as she handed Barbara a bottle to give to Phyllis.

"I'm not FINE!" she said as she took the bottle and put it back down on the table. "She's YOUR baby, not mine! I'm not your live-in babysitter!" Barbara ran outside and sat on the porch step and cried.

"What is that all about?" I asked, but I really did understand how she might have felt. "I think you need to talk with her."

Margret picked up the baby and put the bottle to her lips. Little Phyllis began sucking the bottle and Margret walked outside to console Barbara with the baby in her arms.

"I'm sorry Barbara. I didn't realize that I was forcing you to take care of her," as Margret stood there swaying her body to keep the baby quiet. "I'm just having a hard time right now. This is just too much for me." Margret was beginning to cry. "I need your help, Barbara, please. I love you."

"I love you too, Mom, but I just feel as though you expect me to raise your children while you go off and go to luncheons and gatherings with your friends. What about MY friends? What about MY life?"

"Okay, I'll stay home more often, but will you at least take Neil to the park? He enjoys that and I can't take him and take care of the baby too."

"Sure mom, I can do that," Barbara finally consented, "I'm sorry." She stood up and walked back into the house and went to her bedroom slamming the door behind her.

"But can you watch the kids while I go to the store?" Margret shouted out to Barbara.

"Margret!" I said as I was surprised that she would ask at a time like this.

"Well," she said innocently. "I don't see the problem."

The next morning Barbara agreed to take Neil to the park. The house was quiet as Margret was doing some sewing and I was reading the paper, while Phyllis was asleep in her crib. Barbara came running in the house with Neil, putting him in his playpen and she was excited about something that had just happened. She twirled around in the living room in front of where Margret and I were sitting, and I could see she was getting ready to tell us something with her usual dramatic enthusiasm. She'd make a good actress, I thought to myself.

"Mom, Dad, I have a date!" she said as she handed Neil his stuffed bear. "I was at the park and Neil started crying and fussing and while I was trying to console him, a young man stopped and held up his camera and asked if he could take a photograph of me and MY little boy?" She laughed. "I said, are you kidding! Can't you see he's crying? He then said he was sorry, that he didn't mean to impose. He thought Neil looked so cute with his dark hair and that he looked liked ME! Well, I let him know he's not cute when he's crying and he's not my son, he's my brother!"

I watched Barbara pacing back and forth as she told us what had happened.

"He said, he never thought about that. He apologized and introduced himself as Bill Loescher and he lives in Harrison, and that he likes to come to the park and take pictures of the beach and he saw me and well, he wanted to meet me!" my daughter continued to babble on. "I apologized for snapping at him and told him my name and introduced Neil to him. We shook hands and I did notice he was quite good looking. He's got the bluest eyes and he's muscular, but not too much, and has blonde hair. I told him that I lived just down the street from the park and that I come down there often. We walked down towards the beach and he pushed the stroller onto the pebbled road for me," Barbara continued as

she was elaborating a scene with, "The tide was coming in and the warm breeze felt good as we walked along the shore road near the beach. He's in the Navy and stationed in Washington, DC right now. He's home on leave and will have to go back next week."

As she continued to talk about her afternoon meeting, Barbara seemed like she was in her own little world. She went to the window and looked out as though she was seeing him standing there.

"He then asked, 'this may be too soon, but would you go out for dinner with me sometime?' He stopped the stroller and turned to me and then said, 'I'm hoping that we might get to know each other.' "

Barbara swung around and acted as if she were with him and said, "Um… well… sure, I would

130

love too. I gave him my phone number. He asked me out for Friday night!"

Margret and I were not certain about this date, since we had not met this young man. Barbara was so excited we didn't want to "burst her bubble."

"We walked back to the main road and Bill left me with Neil and the stroller as he walked towards his car. He waved and I waved back and then I crossed the road and hurried back home to tell you – I've got a date, and he's taking me out for dinner on Friday night" she finished on a happy squeal.

My daughter twirled around the room in happiness and Neil tried to imitate her in his playpen.

"Oh, but I was planning to go out to a movie," Margret interrupted.

Barbara's face fell and her spinning came to a stop. "Mom, no, don't you do this to me!"

"Now, don't get upset, Barb, I was just kidding," my wife said, back-tracking a little.

"I'm not so sure you were kidding," Barbara said petulantly. She picked up Neil from the playpen and put him on the floor, and handed him some juice. Then she poured herself a cup of coffee and sat down at the kitchen table, ignoring us. I could tell she was crying and knew she just wanted to be left alone.

Neil continued playing with his stuffed bear, but seemed to have trouble with his eyes as he kept squinting. At first I thought he might have something in his eyes. I started to walk towards him, but he quickly crawled over to the side of the room and began banging his head on the wall. Barbara also noticed and came back into the living room. We all watched Neil for a moment and finally Barbara spoke up.

"Mom, we need to have Neil checked out. That isn't normal," she pointed out as he banged his head against the wall again. "Haven't you noticed that before? I have."

"Well, maybe you're right," Margret said as she watched Neil. "Okay, we'll take him to the doctor and see what's going on," she agreed hastily.

The next day we scheduled an appointment and later test results showed that Neil's eyes were bad and were probably the cause of his headaches and why he was banging his head. After fitting him with prescription glasses, he was able to see and the headaches stopped.

****

In July we decided to make a trip out to the farm to get away for a while. Barbara went along and, of course, was talked into taking care of Neil and Phyllis.

Margret and I worked around the house, sweeping out the dust, and fixing window panes that had been broken by the Hardings, who we had evicted, and cleaning out the well to get the pump working. But my daughter, for some reason, was not comfortable taking care of the baby.

"Mom!" Barbara yelled before long, "The baby seems to be having problems breathing! She doesn't look good!"

"Let me see," my wife said as she picked the baby up and soothed her. "Oh, she's okay; she probably only has allergies to all the dust around here."

"Mom, she scares me!" my daughter pleaded. "Her breathing isn't right. I'm afraid she'll die!"

"Oh, Barbara, you make such a big deal over everything," Margret said dismissively.

"Maybe so, but I don't want to be responsible for her anymore!" Barbara yelled back.

"Well, okay…then maybe it's time for YOU to go back to Rye!" my wife all of a sudden yelled back to Barbara as she pointed to the door.

"What's going on?" I asked as I walked in from outside, unable to stay out of it any longer. "What's all the yelling about?"

"I want Barbara to get out of here!" Margret yelled. "She won't help me out with the children and she has no respect for me! If she won't help, then I want you to take her to the train station and send her back to Rye."

"SURE… if that's what you WANT, I'll be glad to go home!" Barbara yelled back.

Margret took the baby and went into the bedroom, slamming the door behind her.

"What just happened?" I asked my daughter.

"Dad, I just can't do this anymore. I'm not a babysitter for your kids! I want to go home!" Barbara sat down on the sofa and began to cry.

"Can't this be worked out between you two?" I asked as I sat down next to her.

"Not anymore. I don't want to be responsible for your kids. Obviously, mom doesn't understand! I just want to go home."

"Well, at eighteen, you're old enough to be on your own I guess," I said sadly, realizing she wasn't a little girl anymore. "Okay, I'll take you to the train station tomorrow."

"I want to take the train TODAY!" she sobbed. "I want to get out of here!"

"Oh, Barb," I said as I held her. "I love you and I hate seeing you so unhappy. Can't you work this out with your mother?"

"No, I'm done!" she abruptly said.

I went to the desk drawer and pulled out the train schedule and said, "There is a train that leaves out of Nichols tonight at 10:30, but it's a local. It's called the New York Mail Train."

"Good, I'll take it," she said firmly. "I can just sleep all the way to New York."

"Well," I said as I realized what she would have to do. "The train is a local and the last stop is in Hoboken, New Jersey, around 5:30 a.m. From there, you'll need to take the Hudson Tubes to Manhattan."

"What's the Hudson Tubes?" Barbara asked as she wiped her eyes.

"It's like a train that goes under the Hudson River and you'll end up on Sixth Avenue and 33rd Street, which is near Penn Station. You could take the subway from there and switch subways at Times Square to go to Grand Central Station." I thought about all that she would need to remember and do, plus she'd be carrying a suitcase. "Tell you what, let me give you some extra cash and you can take a taxi from Penn Station to Grand Central Station and hopefully you'll catch the train to Rye around 7:30 or 8:00 a.m."

"Sure," she solemnly said. "Thanks dad. I love you and I'm sorry."

Barbara packed her clothes and we headed for the car. Margret wouldn't even come out of the bedroom to say goodbye. I drove Barbara to Nichols that night, where she would catch the Lackawanna local train that would put her into Hoboken, New Jersey, early the next morning. I wrote down what she needed to do when she arrived in Hoboken. I gave her plenty of money for the expenses. When Barbara got on the train, she sat down in a window seat and looked out at me and waved. I stood there on the platform and waved back and threw her a kiss. I could see that Barbara was beginning to cry and turned away as the train pulled away from the station. I felt heartbroken that she had left in such an unsettling way. As I drove back to the house, I started thinking: How could I fix this? How could I get Margret and Barbara to work things out for them? Oh, I miss my sweet daughter already. Breath… just breath. I took a good long slow breath to calm myself down before getting out of the car to deal with Margret's emotional state.

I had been listening to the radio when I heard the announcer say: *Saturday, July 28, 1945. A B-25 Bomber crashed into the Empire State Building! William Franklin Smith, Jr., was piloting the plane on a routine personnel transport mission from Bedford Army Air Field to Newark Airport. Smith asked for clearance to land, but was advised of zero visibility. Proceeding anyway, he became disoriented by the fog, and started turning right instead of left after passing the Chrysler Building. At 9:40 a.m., the aircraft crashed into the north side of the Empire State Building, between the 78th and 80th floors, carving an 18 by 20 foot hole in the building where the offices of the National Catholic Welfare Council were located. One engine shot through the south side opposite the impact and flew as far as the next block, dropping 900 feet and landing on the roof of a nearby building and starting a fire that destroyed a penthouse. The other engine and part of the landing gear plummeted down an elevator shaft. The resulting fire was extinguished in forty minutes. Fourteen people were killed: Smith, the two others aboard the bomber, along with eleven people in the building. Stay tune for more information at our 6:00 hour.*

I was aghast and instantly worried for my daughter. "Margret! Come here! Did you hear the news on the radio?"

"No, I've been busy with the kids," she said tiredly when she joined me in the living room.

"A plane hit the Empire State Building. I hope Barbara is okay."

"Oh, I'm sure she's fine," she said without as much concern in her voice as I would have thought she would show.

"I'm going to call Barbara and make sure she's okay," I said determinedly.

"Sure, do what you need to do," my wife said, walking out of the room.

I anxiously called the Rye phone number, and was relieved to hear Barbara answer the phone. She was fine there, and safe. She was surprised that I'd called until I told her why, and she was glad she hadn't been there when it happened. My daughter had been able to catch the New Haven commuter train to Rye before all the commotion and Bill met her at the Rye Station and brought her home.

"How's mom?" Barbara finally asked. "Has she calmed down? Do you think she'll ever speak to me again?"

"Give her time," I said, trying to sound casual. "It takes her a while to forgive and forget."

The baby was getting much worse, so we decided to take the younger children back to Rye to get Phyllis some medical treatment. I also wanted to face Barbara and figure out a way to resolve the problems between her and her mother, but, after being home for a couple of days, it was still quiet around the house. Nothing was said about the incident at the farm, because nothing was said between them. When Margret was upset she can give you the "silent" treatment and that can last a while.

After about a week of silence between my wife and daughter, Barbara finally decided to do something about it. She stood in the middle of the room, clearing her throat, and said, "Mom, Dad, it's time for me to be on my own."

"What do you mean?" Margret asked, startled out of her silence.

"I need to start my own life, to find out what I can do or be. I plan to find a job and get an apartment," Barbara replied.

"But I thought you were happy here."

"No, YOU were happy that I was here to be your in-house babysitter!" Barbara said, with her voice rising, "I…"

Margret interrupted with, "Now Barbara, I'm sorry about that. I didn't realize that your sister and brother were such a burden to you."

"You just don't understand, do you?" Barbara explained with tears in her eyes. "I love them, but I don't think it's up to me to raise them." My daughter threw up her hands and left the room.

A week went by, and Barbara and Margret hardly spoke to each other. I was hoping the situation would resolve itself, but Barbara moved out of the house at Ridgeland Terrace into her own place, an apartment in Rye and started a job at the local Rye National Bank as a teller. She continued to babysit now and then, but it was on her own terms. During the times Barbara consented to watch the children, she would tell us some of the things happening in her life. She told us that Bill Loescher, the sailor she'd met while with Neil in the park, would visit her on every leave from the Navy. They spent as much time as they could together. When he was gone, they wrote or called.

One late afternoon, Bill and Barbara came by for a visit. She told us, with suppressed excitement, that she and Bill had gone for a walk in the park and that he had stopped her at the exact spot where they had met. I could see it coming as she was dramatizing the incident. Bill got into the excitement as well.

"I took her hands and held them in my hands," Bill said as he again held her hands. "We looked at each other and I asked her to marry me."

"Yes! Oh Yes!" Barbara answered. "He grabbed me and swung me around and we laughed."

"She said YES!" Bill interrupted.

Barbara ended by shouting happily, "We're getting married!"

Margret and I stood there with grins on our faces, I said, "We were hoping you would say yes."

"How did you know?" Barbara asked surprised.

"Bill was polite enough to ask our permission," I answered and was glad he asked.

I gave Barbara a big hug and shook Bill's hand, "We're so happy for you."

"Thanks Daddy."

"So when are you two planning to marry?" Margret asked.

"Bill needs to go back to Washington, DC, after the Christmas holidays, so we decided to get married just before Christmas. We think we can make arrangements with the church for December 23rd."

"We can have a small reception here at the house," Margret suggested. "It will be so pretty with the Christmas decorations."

Bill and Barbara laughed as they told us the story of when they went to the Rye Courthouse to get their marriage license. "Neil was standing next to me and I was holding Phyllis in my arms as I filled out the paperwork." Barbara said.

Bill spoke up. "People at the courthouse looked at us and I'm sure they were thinking, It's about time they got married." Barbara and Bill laughed again.

The time flew by, and soon it was December 23, 1945. At the Rye Presbyterian Church, I escorted Barbara down the aisle. Neil stood up in the pew next to Margret and yelled out, "Big Sis, where are you going!"

"Neil, sit down," Margret said embarrassed, as she pulled him down into his seat.

The congregation chuckled slightly as we continued down the aisle. I presented my daughter to Bill. She took his hand and the ceremony began. It was short and sweet, and the reception afterwards was just right. After the next couple of days Barbara and Bill moved to Washington, DC, where they stayed until his time in the Navy was over in March of 1946. We missed seeing Barbara and hoped that they might move back near Rye to settle down. I was glad that Margret and Barbara were back to speaking with each other. Barbara would call occasionally and the two women would chat for a while.

April of 1946, Bill and Barbara did move back into a small apartment on Purchase Street in Rye. It was a second floor walkup and had only one bedroom and a bath, but for a newlywed couple it was wonderful. Bill, with the help of his friends, made some major improvements to the building, including redoing the roof. The repairs he did for the building owner lowered their rent. Bill was able to get a good job as a die-toolmaker with Ward Leonard Electric Company. They enjoyed their life as newlyweds and confided they were hoping to have a family of their own. Barbara was able to get her job back at the to help save for a down payment to build their home.

Margret and I were looking at making a change for ourselves – we wanted to stop renting and buy a house in Rye. We contacted a realtor and soon were house-hunting.

"We sure have looked at a lot of houses lately," I said a couple of weeks into the search. "I hope we haven't been too demanding with what we want. I would like our house to be halfway between the elementary school and the high school, and have a nice yard for the children to play in."

The real estate agent found the perfect house. We made an offer on a four bedroom Dutch Colonial that had been built in 1923 and sat on three-quarters of an acre on the corner of Rye Beach Avenue and Elmwood Avenue. Large maple trees shaded the front yard and the spacious backyard had a little playhouse on the far corner. It was a perfect place for the kids. The offer was accepted, and we waited eagerly for the closing. One evening while taking care of a late diapering, Margret heard sirens and people yelling outside.

"Hurry, get the hose hooked up!" a fireman yelled, "This old wooden garage is going up like match sticks and catching the trees on fire!"

"Van," Margret yelled! "Get up! There's a fire across the road. The leaves of the trees are burning and headed this way!"

I'd blearily heard the commotion, but I jumped out of bed and quickly got dressed when Margret yelled. My wife gathered up Neil and Phyllis and put blankets around each one.

"Hurry!" I said, looking out the window as I tried to gather what I could into a suitcase. "It's getting closer to us!"

The fire made the whole area light up, and flames seemed to hover over everything. The firemen scrambled around with their hoses spraying water furiously, but the fire still grew.

"Here, throw some stuff in that box!" Margret pointed to a cardboard box that Neil had been playing with the day before. "Get some of the children's clothes and their stuffed toys. Here, put some of our clothes in there too!" she quickly handed me handfuls of clothes from the closet and dresser. I didn't even know what I was putting in the box or suitcase. I just stuffed them in as quickly as I could. I grabbed some of my artwork and supplies and I threw everything in the trunk of the car, while Margret put the children in the back seat before getting in herself. We packed and were out of there within ten minutes as the fire kept growing.

"Where are we going to go?" Margret asked as I slid into the driver's seat.

"There's a motel in Mamaroneck. We can stay there for tonight," I replied as we headed out with other evacuees. "We'll come back in the morning to see if our place is still here."

The next morning, we drove back to Ridgeland Terrace, and despite the smell of smoke everywhere, our house had not been damaged by the fire. It was scary to find out that the garage and part of the house just across the street were badly burned and to see the leaves on the trees were gone.

"I'll be glad when we can get into our new house," Margret said as she got the children back into the house and started some breakfast.

When the real estate closing papers finally went through not long afterwards, we moved into our own place. We lived two blocks from Rye Park, walking distance to the beach where we could go swimming in Long Island Sound and we were close to Playland Amusement Park.

The house needed some renovations, but we were used to hard work after all the things we had done to the farm. We began by knocking out a wall that separated the living room and dining room to make a long L-shaped living room. On the small end of the 'L' was a stone fireplace. I added bookcases, and later, a small washroom.

The house had double deck porches on each end, allowing us to sit out there to enjoy the cool breeze of summer in the evenings. We could also watch the fireworks from the amusement park on Friday and Saturday nights from our upstairs porch. Occasionally, we would take the children to Playland. Margret would push Phyllis in the stroller to a bench and sit down and watch while I took Neil to the merry-go-round or the little train that circled Playland. The smell of cotton candy, hot dogs, and the salt air from Long Island Sound made for a nice occasional afternoon away from the renovation work.

On top of the house repairs, my freelance artwork was keeping me busy and with two young children running around, I was at the point of needing my own studio to work in. After drawing out a plan on where and how I wanted my studio, I decided to make a deal with Barbara's husband, Bill. I asked him to come over and suggested to Bill, "If you would help me build my studio, in return, I will help you with the building materials for your home."

"Sounds like a great plan," Bill agreed, and we talked over the details of what supplies we would need.

I showed Margret and Barbara the plan and noted, "Where our back porch is now, the upper porch floor will become the roof that will cover my studio," I explained. "I'll put in a back door to my studio that will go out to the extended porch. Oh, and there will be French doors separating my studio from the living room. What do you think?"

"That's a large undertaking, Van," Margret said. "But knowing you, it will get done."

The summer months were busy with the building and keeping up with work. Bill and I worked well together. Bill was muscular and could handle some of the heavy lifting of boards and beams without me. I ended up leaving a lot of the work for Bill to do while I continued with my artwork and commuting to New York City almost everyday by train. My work brought the money in to pay for the supplies for my studio as well as giving Bill some much needed extra income. The finished product was a large studio, with the North light coming in through a wall of louvered windows. I had six, four-drawer file cabinets added which were built into one of the walls. It's when I added my drawing board, easel, and my other art furniture and materials that it finally looked like MY studio.

"What do you think, Margret," I asked as I opened the French doors to let her see the finished studio.

"This is really nice, Van," she said as she looked around. "I like the porch out there too. You and Bill really did a wonderful job."

I enjoyed working in my own studio, and yet I was close to family when I needed to be. Margret tried to keep the children out of the studio, which I appreciated. Some evenings, we would go out onto the back porch, but it would get too hot in the summer months with no roof over the porch, so we added a large awning which made the back porch a perfect place to sit with ocean breezes cooling us in the warm afternoons.

Fall of 1947, Barbara came to visit us one afternoon to announce some exciting news.

"I have been waiting for some time and actually I was a little worried that it might not happen. Bill and I have been married for three years now, but guess what? I'm PREGNANT!"

"Oh Barb, I'm so happy for you," Margret said as she hugged Barbara. "I knew you were concerned, but I didn't want to say anything. Oh my goodness, that means I'm going to be a grandmother!"

Barbara seemed to be handling her pregnancy quite well. She even glowed and was looking forward to becoming a mother. She told us she had set up a little area in their bedroom for the new arrival with a cute bassinet and a table that she could use to change the baby's diapers. She was "nesting" and invited us to come and see what she had done to get prepared.

"I am so ready!" she said to Margret and me, as she placed some little stuffed animals in the crib. "I hope I've got everything I need."

July 12th of 1948, Barbara had her first child at United Hospital in Port Chester, a little girl they named Willa Susan Loescher, and my wife and I couldn't have been prouder.

"Barbara has her own child to take care of and we are now grandparents! I hope she doesn't need me to babysit," Margret said confidentially. "I've got enough with our two kids."

Bill owned property on Davenport Street, which was right next to his parent's home in Harrison, New York and began working on his own home. He showed me his design for a Cape Cod style house with two bedrooms upstairs and a bathroom. Downstairs was a small living room, kitchen, a small eating area and a back porch. Bill kept busy with building and also with his regular job as a die-toolmaker. The house was completed in time for them to move in with their new child and later that year Barbara found out she was pregnant again.

"Again!" Margret said. "You're sure popping them out!"

September of 1949, they had another little girl named Linda Barbara Loescher. I was glad that they were settled in their new home in Harrison. Margret loved how Barbara decorated it with cute gingham curtains in the kitchen and lace curtains in the living room. She had placed little country knick-knacks here and there, a cuckoo clock and some of my paintings on the wall. She planted rose bushes in the front yard and a vegetable garden in the back. My daughter had her dream home. Having two little girls kept Barbara busy. Occasionally when we visited, we would all sit out on their back porch and listen to the crickets and discussed the day as we watched the children... our children and now our grandchildren.

Margret and I missed making trips to the farm, but with having two young children and with my work, there just wasn't time. We tried to stay in touch with the Huddles and as far as we knew, Windhill Farms was still standing. We weren't ready to sell it or give up on it. We still kept thinking we would move out there and retire someday after the children were grown.

In 1950, I was offered a steady job with Batton, Barton, Durstin, & Osborn Advertising (better known as BBDO in the advertising world) in New York City. I would be illustrating magazine ads for clients such as: Motorola TV, Lucky Strike Cigarettes, Schenley Whiskey, and Ford

Automobiles. I commuted the forty-five minute train ride five days a week from Rye and did magazine illustrations at home on the weekends for Collier, Redbook and the Saturday Evening Post. Margret kept busy with Neil and Phyllis and even got involved in Cub Scouts with Neil. I helped out when it was time to take them on camping trips.

When it drew closer to Christmas time that year, I had already decided I wanted to give Neil his own train set. I assembled a ping pong table in the basement and began converting it to a "train" table. I bought miniature buildings, houses, bridges, little tiny people, and an electric train that had lights and a whistle. I spent many evenings, leading up to the big day, constructing and making sure the train would run on the winding tracks through tunnels and over bridges. It was quite elaborate and I was so proud of it.

"I can't wait to see Neil's expression when he sees this!" I excitedly said as I blew the whistle from the switch below the table.

"I'm putting a little wooden train in his stocking," Margret said. "He'll think that's the train he's getting."

"Great idea!"

"I still need to wrap Phyllis' doll." Margret said as she wrapped presents and put bows on top of each one.

"Look!" Margret said as she watched snow falling outside the window, "Guess we're going to have a white Christmas!"

"Come on kids, we need to go out and get a Christmas tree!" I said. "It's Christmas Eve and this is the best time to find one."

Phyllis and Neil were so excited. They giggled at the thought that Christmas would be the next day. I enjoyed getting the tree on Christmas Eve, because I had my own system on how to buy a tree. When we arrived at the Christmas tree lot in Rye, they only had a few trees left.

"Okay, kids, see which tree you would like to take home."

They wandered around and spotted a tree that they liked. Then I asked the man in charge, "How much for this tree?" as I pointed to one that was bigger than the one the children had chosen.

"Five dollars," he replied.

"Oh, well how about this one?" and I pointed to the tree they wanted.

"Five dollars."

"But this one is smaller and doesn't have enough branches on the bottom," I complained.

"Well, okay, three dollars," the man offered.

"How about a dollar?" I asked.

"A dollar!" the man complained. "How about two dollars?"

"I'll give you a dollar-fifty and you throw in a couple of extra branches," I said as I handed him the money.

"Okay, okay, you win," he finally consented. "It's Christmas Eve and I want to go home."

I tied the tree to the top of the car and drove home, presenting Margret with a fairly decent tree. I put it in the tree stand and placed it in the studio, and I attached the extra branches where needed with string to fill in the bare places. The children and I spent the evening decorating the tree with lights and ornaments. Margret was busy decorating cookies in the kitchen. The house smelled of Christmas with the scent of freshly baked cookies and the spruce Christmas tree. When we heard Christmas carolers outside, we opened the front door to listen. The snow was falling around the carolers as they sang, "Silent Night, Holy Night….." before moving on into the night, still singing. When it was bedtime, it was a bit of a struggle to get the kids to bed, but finally the house was quiet after closing their bedroom doors. Margret and I went to the studio, sat down on the small sofa, cuddled, and stared at the beautiful Christmas tree enjoying our moment together in silence.

Christmas morning arrived and the children were awake before dawn, running into our bedroom screaming, "It's CHRISTMAS!" They jumped on the bed and yelled, "Come on, come on!"

"Wait a minute," I said as I put my robe on. "We've got to make sure that Santa was here."

Margret and the children waited at the top of the staircase as I walked down the stairs. A pinkish glow came on as I turned on the Christmas tree lights in the studio. I put Christmas music on the radio and finally yelled out, "Yup, Santa has been here!"

The children ran downstairs screaming "It's Christmas!" and began unwrapping packages. Phyllis began playing with her new doll and a wooden horse that had real horse hair covering it. Neil played with an erector set and a toy truck. Margret checked out a wool hat and scarf and was excited over a nice watch I'd given her. As for myself, I found some new shirts, a wool vest, and a pipe.

"Don't forget to check the stockings!" Margret said as we went into the living room by the fireplace.

I had started a fire in the fireplace during the time the children were unwrapping their presents. The glow and heat warmed the room. Each stocking was filled with candy and fruit and one small present. Phyllis came across a candy cane and began sucking on it and then found a small wooden horse and began pretending it was running across the room as she carried it. Neil came across the little wooden train and began rolling it on the floor making train sounds, "Toot, toot!"

I snuck away to the basement, turned on lights and powered up the electric train. I was down there for a while, making sure everything was in running order. The little lights on the inside of the coaches were lit up, the whistle blew on cue and the railroad guard went up and down making the red lights blink as the train went over the crossroad on the tracks. "Everything is working, it's ready!"

Feeling excited, I came back up stairs and said to Neil. "Come on down stairs and play with your new train set."

Neil continued to play with his wooden train and quietly said, "That's okay dad. You play with your train and I'll play with mine."

The summer of 1950, we took a weeks vacation and drove out to the Windhill Farms with Neil and Phyllis. The grass was waist high on our spread and some house windows had been broken out, but it was still good to see the place again. We had to rough it at the main house, since we had the electricity cut off while we had been gone and the well had to be cleaned out before we could get fresh water. Neil and Phyllis loved the place and explored the house and the barns. But the second night, Phyllis had trouble breathing. We immediately took her to Doc Brown in Nichols, and decided that she had asthma.

"She may be allergic to the house dust or mold from the old farmhouse, or maybe the grasses growing around it?" Doc Brown informed us as he gave her some cough syrup to help with her coughing. "It might be best that you go back to Rye where the salt air from the ocean is better for her."

Sadly, but quickly, we packed up and left right away. Back in Rye, the next morning, Doctor Pennick came to examine Phyllis. He gave her an adrenaline injection and some cough syrup.

"The injection I gave her will open up the airways, but she'll feel a little jittery. You need to keep her quiet for a few days," the doctor informed us as he was leaving. "Give her the cough syrup every four hours and that will bring up some of the mucus."

For the next few days we had to keep her in bed with extra pillows to keep her propped upright. We hadn't expected that something like that would happen, and hoped it was a one-time thing. But each time we tried to go to the farm, at different parts of the year, we would end up driving back to Rye because of Phyllis' asthma.

In 1951, we decided to vacation at 'Lake O'Meadows,' which was near Warren Center, not too far from our farm, because we wanted to see if the area made a difference in Phyllis. Small cabins surrounded the lake and could be rented for five dollars a night. The cabin had two small bedrooms, a bathroom and a large living room, that was also the kitchen, and a porch overlooking the lake. When it rained we could hear the rain on the tin roof, which was quite loud, but we even got used to that. The lake was set between rolling hills. There were boats to row and rental horses to ride. Phyllis was okay there and loved the horses. Even at six years old, she could ride on her own and spent most of the day on a horse while Neil, on the other hand, preferred swimming in the lake.

One afternoon, we decided we would all go horseback riding. Margret and I didn't ride much, but we wanted to explore the area. Phyllis led the way, since she already knew all the trails and fields to ride in.

"Come on, let's go!" she kept saying as she trotted up ahead of us eager to show us everything. She took us to the top of a hill that overlooked the lake and the cabins. It was a sight worth the ride although I was sore the next morning. But our stay at Lake O'Meadows made it clear to my wife and me that it was something on the farm itself, and not the lands around Windham Center, that was bad for Phyllis.

I drove to Windham Farms on some of the days while Margret and the kids were busy at the lake. I swept out the place, washed windows and floors, and cleared out dust, mold, and mildew. Margret and I thought that maybe if the farmhouse were completely clean that we could return to the farm with Phyllis, but it was too big a job to do by myself in the few days we had. It made me sad to realize because I missed living there. When I drove back to the lake, I told Margret how things were at the farm, but we both understood that now wasn't the time to try again at Windham Farms.

****

Back in Rye the farm got pushed aside again because business was picking up for me. That fall of 1951, I received a letter from a publishing company, about illustrating the book *The Three Musketeers.*

"This will keep me busy," I told Margret "I'm not sure how I can do this, but the money sure would help." I showed Margret the letter from Grosset & Dunlap Publishers.

Dear Mr. Van Swearingen;

Norman Price had done a great deal of research in preparation for doing the illustrations for the book The Three Musketeers and had done many of the illustrations. Unfortunately, on August 2, 1951 he died.

A great deal of research was still to be done and additional drawings to be made.

We would like to commission you to complete the assignment, and we feel that you would be able to come up with what is needed to complete the book. Your style and technique are similar to Mr. Price's paintings and we hope that you will consider the offer.

I mailed a reply accepting the commission, suggesting a timeframe and fee. The publisher agreed and the work started when I received more notes from the publisher in the mail.

"This isn't going to be easy," I said to my wife as I looked at what I had been given, and what still needed to be done. "Norman Price had started the research and completed sketches, but after he died, all his friends and well wishers came and cleaned out his studio. All his research papers, notes, and photographs have disappeared."

"Do you think you can do it?" Margret asked. "How are you going to continue working at

BBDO Advertising Agency and also take on this project? I hope you don't regret this."

"It will take me months of research before I can even get started." I moaned. "I need to study the costumes of the 1600's and know enough about them to be able to design clothes for all the characters in the book. Also, I need to look at the buildings and décor in France and the swords they used, and yes, I want to do this."

I used neighbors and friends and even my daughter Barbara as models for the illustrations. I was able to obtain some costumes and headgear for them to wear and bought a couple of swords from a pawn shop for props. One afternoon, Barbara came by for a visit to see how the illustrations were coming along.

"Oh Dad, is that me sitting in that chair?" Barbara asked, observed one of the paintings. "I'd wondered why I'd had to sit like that."

"You had no idea all that action was going to happen behind you, did you?" I teased her.

"It makes me want to read the book!" she said as she looked and studied the sword fight going on behind the chair where the character she had modeled for was passed out. "You've got so much detail in this painting."

Her words made me feel good, because I wanted the illustrations to be as accurate as possible. It was a challenge to find information about the area of France and the time period of the story. I had even managed to find one painting of a building under construction that really happened at that time, which was helpful. I also executed some pen and ink drawings for the book, working to match the style of Norman Price, but the paintings took months. When I finally submitted my work I was pleased that no changes needed to be made. I received a nice sum of money for my work. I slated some for the farm's use.

Financially, after this commission, we were in great shape, so I bought myself a sailboat. I'd always loved to sail and had done a lot of it when Margret and I lived in Buenos Aires. At first I kept the nineteen foot sailboat moored in Milton Harbor in Rye and had to row my dingy, which I also purchased, to the boat. My wife and I later joined the Coveleigh Club in Rye. I moved my boat to be moored there, and Margret enjoyed sitting on the beach that overlooked Long Island Sound. My wife liked the idea of belonging to a beach club, and she would visit with the other mothers while watching Neil and Phyllis swim and play.

Living in Rye, NY, especially with Phyllis' asthma, really was the best place for us while raising two young children. In the morning, after breakfast, Margret would tell them to go out and play. "Just be home by 5:15 before your father gets home from work."

Our neighborhood was full of families with young kids. It was nice watching the children play hop-scotch or jumping rope or other games. Phyllis loved her backyard playhouse that had come with the property, and she would invite other girls over to pretend to have tea. Neil and Phyllis would ride their bikes around the neighborhood. Sometimes they would go to the beach to play or a group of kids would build tree houses in the local woods or maybe just ride their bikes to the corner store to get a Popsicle. We never worried about what could happen to them.

Chapter 10

One More Time with Family

The summer of 1954, we decided to make a trip Windhill Farms – or rather, its immediate vicinity. We contacted the Huddles to see if we could stay with them, since the farmhouse was probably not the best place to stay because of Phyllis' asthma.

"We'd love to see ya folks!" Grace said in reply to our asking. "What about Barbara, is she coming too?"

"Well," I answered. "She now has a family of her own. I think Margret had written to you about her two girls."

"We'd love to see them! You know we have plenty of room in this here house."

"I'll ask her and see if she can bring her family. Thanks Grace."

When I hung up with Grace I immediately called Barbara and asked, "Would you like to go out to the farm for a visit? It would only be for a week. The Huddles said they would love to see you and we could all stay at their house."

"Are you sure?" Barbara asked me, "What about the kids?"

"Children are included!"

Barbara said she'd talk to Bill about it and get back to me. When she did, it turned out that Bill had to work, but she said that he thought it was a good idea for Barbara to get away and for the kids to see the farm. We made our plans accordingly.

The Oldsmobile had given up the ghost a while ago, so I had purchased a bright blue Kaiser-Fraser automobile. With three adults and four kids, plus our suitcases, the car was packed when it was time to leave for Pennsylvania. We arrived late that afternoon and right away the children explored some of the smaller sheds and barns, finding chickens, pigs, horses and cows. My granddaughter, Linda had broken her arm a couple of weeks before our trip, thanks to a neighbor child who had pushed her off of a stone wall. She had just turned five and her older sister Willa was six. My daughter Phyllis was nine and my son Neil was twelve. As they romped away, it struck me as something of a surprise to realize that my younger children and my grandchildren were all roughly the same age.

Neil showed the younger kids around like a tour guide and pretended to know everything about the farm. Fortunately, the Huddles' house was quite large and could accommodate all of us. With four large bedrooms upstairs and beyond a closed door, through a narrow hallway, were four more bedrooms. Years ago, the house was an Inn.

Grace had mentioned that during the Civil War, soldiers were hidden in those back bedrooms.

The children loved the bathroom upstairs. "Look, Daddy," Neil announced and laughed. "You can see through the vent in the floor and see into the kitchen. We can listen to your conversations." The vent let heat in from the kitchen to help heat the bathroom. The house was full of secret spaces like the back staircase, which was steep and narrow and opened into the kitchen.

I loved the main staircase with its beautiful oak carvings on the railings. It reminded me of my father and how he made a living out of doing this type of wood carving for staircases and for trims around doorways.

Off of the living room were two bedrooms, one small one for Donald, the other larger room where Grace and Ned slept. From the living room, you would walk through the dining room and then into the large kitchen. Margret liked the kitchen. I understood why, it was light and airy with a long table in the middle with plenty of chairs around it. An old wood cook stove stood on the far side of the kitchen that hadn't been used for years, an electric stove was on the opposite side and always was in use. Off the kitchen was another room with a laundry tub, storage area, pantry, a large deep sink, and a toilet over in the corner of the room, just sitting there with no walls around it.

Barbara was especially happy to see Donald, and he enjoyed talking with Barbara and teased her just like old times. Although he was completely blind, he knew who she was by the sound of her voice. He was running the farm and yes, even drove the tractor in the fields... only in the fields.

"Yep, we've got 'bout 100 Holstein cows now and some new calves," Donald informed me. "I've got a system on how to feed 'em and milk 'em that works for me."

Even though Ned was in his seventies, he still helped with the farm chores. Between the two of them, they were able to make a profit from milking their cows.

"Sorry we haven't done anything with yur place," Ned apologized, "We keep pretty busy 'round here."

"Oh, we understand," I said. "I'm sorry that we didn't come out more often to try and keep things in shape. We stopped by the main house and it didn't look too bad, but the bees have taken over the little house."

During further conversation we learned that Junia, their daughter, was now teaching in Nichols.

"I teach French!" she said. "Can you just see all these country kids speaking French?" She chuckled, but it was clear she felt as though the kids really liked the language. She even planned a trip to take a few of them to Paris, later in the year.

The children kept busy. Willa, Linda and Phyllis loved the wrap-around porch and would sit on the steps to play games. It was nice to hear them laugh and sing together. Neil enjoyed checking out the farm equipment and watched Donald do some of his chores. Later while Willa and Linda were taking naps, Barbara, Neil, Phyllis and, I went exploring. We walked down to the barn that stored hay and began playing among the hay bales, laughing as we chased each other from one bale to the other.

"Ahhhh!" Phyllis cried out, falling head first between two bales of hay. She screamed, "Get me out of here!"

I pulled her out and brushed the hay out her hair and off her clothes. "Are you okay?" I asked.

"I'm okay, but that was scary," Phyllis said with a quiver in her voice.

"I guess it was," Barbara said soothingly. Looking over at Neil and me, she said, "Let's all get down off this hay and head back towards the house. We've had enough excitement for one day."

Each morning, Grace had Barbara and her children help with feeding the chickens and gathering eggs. Willa and Linda thought that was so much fun and loved seeing the new born chicks. Barbara and her daughters went down to the vegetable garden to help Grace gathered fresh vegetables for dinner.

While they were absorbed doing that, Margret and I decided to walk with Neil and Phyllis over to Windham Farms to look at the house and barns. I looked up the hill, past the barns, and surveyed the field and woods.

"Let's walk to the top of our hill." I suggested.

"It is a clear day. I bet we could see for miles and miles up there," Margret agreed. "Come on kids, we're going for a hike."

It took us a good thirty minutes walking up the steep pasture to get to the edge of the field. Then we made our way through the dense forest and came to a clearing at the top of the mountain.

"Oh, I forgot how beautiful it is up here," Margret observed. "Look, we can even see Windham Center and over there is Nichols. Oh I just love it up here. I feel like we're on top of the world."

It was beautiful to see the mountains. The color changed from one mountain to the other with greens, blues and purples, reminding me of a pastel drawing with the colors blending and getting lighter and lighter to depict distance. The scattering of wild flowers in the green of the pasture and even the smell of sweet honeysuckle in the air made it perfect. The countryside was what it was all about, and I wanted to breathe it all in. We stayed up there long enough to pick some wild berries, with Phyllis picking some daisies and purple wildflowers as well. We walked down the hill and made our way back to the Huddles and told Barbara about our excursion.

"Oh, I wish that I could have gone. I loved going up there when I was living here." Barbara said as she poured a glass of juice for Willa. "Maybe when my kids are a little older we can walk up there."

"Does that mean you'll be coming back?" Grace asked. "I would love to have you folks come visit again. We've had so much fun this week."

"I'm sure we'll be coming back from time to time if you let us," I said. "It might not be an all-summer stay, but maybe a week. We wouldn't want to impose on you. We can stay at our place or maybe at Lake O'Meadows, where the kids loved the horseback riding and swimming in the lake. You could visit with us there as well as us visiting you here."

The next day, as I was walking towards the milking barn, I saw my son Neil across the road imitating a large bull. He was intrigued by this huge black cow and stood looking at it. The cow started mooing at Neil, put its head down and pawed the ground. Neil did the same thing, teasing it. That made me realize that it wasn't a cow, but a bull!

"Neil!" I yelled "Don't tease that bull!" I was afraid the bull, enraged, might charge and hurt my boy.

Neil, thankfully, stopped. "Daddy, why is he chained like that?" my son pointed to the long chain that was attached to a ring in the bull's nose. The other end of the chain attached to a large stake in the ground in the open field.

"He's a bull and he's been separated from the cows for now," I explained.

"Did he do something wrong?"

"Well, no, but he can get out-of-hand and this way he won't hurt anybody. Don't tease him!"

"Oh, okay. Can I come with you?"

"Sure," I said in relief. "Let's see what Donny is doing."

We walked to the cow barn to see Donald. The smell of cow paddy, hay and whatever else was in the barn was over-powering, and flies were swarming everywhere, but we figured he was here because we could hear the radio playing country music.

I wanted to make sure that Donald knew we were standing in the doorway, so I asked, "Are the cows producing plenty of milk?" I realized as soon as I said it that it was sort of a stupid question and wished I'd thought of something else.

"Yep," Donald replied, "we get plenty of milk 'round here. I've got twenty-five cows right here in the barn being fed and milked and then when they're done, I'll bring in the next twenty-five."

Neil and I watched Donald place the feed and hay for each cow and noticed he had missed one. I wondered, How on earth does he do all of that when he's completely blind?

I was about to say something about the cow he'd missed, when Donald walked back to where the cow was and put the feed and hay in the feed trough.

"How did you know which cow you missed?" I asked.

"Oh that's easy, I could hear which one wasn't munchin."

One by one, Donald attached the milking machines to the cow's udders. The machines began milking each cow, but the cows didn't seem to mind as they were too busy eating. While that was going on, Donald took the hose and washed the manure down a long ditch that went the whole length of the barn. Then he washed the manure out of the barn to have it clean for the next group of cows.

171

"Barbara has a nice family," Donald commented as he was finishing up the hosing. "I bet she's a good mama."

My mind flashed back to how Donald and Barbara had made eyes at each other when we first moved to Windhill Farms.

"Yes, she certainly is," I answered carefully. "Barbara and her husband Bill seem to be happy."

"That's good." Donald replied without much concern about it.

"Her husband Bill is a hard worker. He built their house and helped me with building my studio."

"That's nice."

"I'm sorry he couldn't come for the week, but he had to work."

"Yeah, that's the way it goes."

"Daddy," Neil interrupted all of a sudden. "Why are the cats lined up over there?"

I turned, thankful for the interruption, and saw three cats all in a line, watching Donald carefully. Donald walked closer to where the cats were, cocked an ear in their direction, and then unhooked one of the milking machines from a nearby cow. He put his hand around the cows' utter and aimed it right at the cats. The cats licked the milk coming at them. Neil and I laughed at the sight and couldn't believe that Donald could aim the stream of milk right at the cats. This seemed to be an ongoing practice with Donald and the barn cats, and they didn't seem to mind their faces being covered with milk.

"We'll catch up later, Donald," I said, letting him know we were going. "Come on Neil, let's go back to the house," and I took a hold of Neil's hand and led him out of the barn.

When we arrived at the house, Grace, Margret and Barbara were getting dinner ready. The kitchen smelled of baked chicken. Margret was snapping beans, Barbara was peeling potatoes and Grace was busy making some homemade biscuits. On the table was a freshly baked apple pie. When it was time for dinner, what city folks call 'lunch,' the long kitchen table was full of food. We even had homemade ice cream to put on top of the pie.

"It's wonderful having ya folks here with us," Grace said as she passed the biscuits. "We have missed ya. I'm so glad ya could come, Barbara, and that we could meet yur children."

"This has been such a wonderful week for me and my girls," Barbara replied. "Thank you so much."

"We love coming here and wish we could stay forever," Margret added.

"Give these girls some of that milk," Grace said as she handed the glass bottle of fresh milk to Margret. "Give 'em the cream part of that bottle, the part that's on top of the rest of the milk, it's good for 'em."

Margret poured the cream into the children's glasses, which was the first time having it for them, and they all loved it. They drank their milk quickly.

"Wish we could get fresh milk like this at home," Margret said as she poured herself some milk.

"What do you folks like to do in Rye?" Grace asked.

"Well, we bought a sailboat," I replied. "We take it out on weekends on Long Island Sound. I've even gotten interested in racing it with other sailors who have the same kind of boat, which is called a Lightning. It's a nineteen foot long sloop and we've been enjoying it."

"You've been enjoying it," Margret interrupted me. "I'm not sure about the rest of us."

"What do you mean by that?" I asked, perplexed.

"It can be scary at times. Remember that storm that came up and the wind was blowing really hard and the boat was heeling so far over? I thought we were going to capsize!"

"But we didn't."

"But we had two small children with us. What would have happened if we had capsized?" she asked.

174

I was surprised, Margret hadn't said anything bad about our times on the boat ever before.

"Oh Margret, it wasn't that dangerous," I said, trying to reassure her.

"Maybe not for you!" she retorted.

"Well, as I was saying," I continued, turning back to Grace. "It's something that we do now and then together."

The next couple days were full of laughter and long talks, but it finally came to the day that it was time to go back home to Rye. As we packed the car, Grace gave us a basket of apples and some strawberry preserves to take back home with us.

"Now ya folks drive safe," Grace said. "We want ya to come visit us again."

"Let's hope it's sooner and not later," I answered as I closed the car door and adjusted the rear view mirror.

"Thanks for putting us up for the week," Barbara said to her.

"We sure did enjoy having ya folks and seein' your cute little girls," Grace replied, waving good-bye.

Everybody waved as the car started down the dirt road. Then it was quiet as we approached our farm.

I slowed down so we could see the farmhouse, the barns and the beautiful mountains surrounding us.

"Stop the car!" Margret said. "I just want to get out and stand here for a minute."

I stopped in front of Windhill Farms main house and we all got out of the car. We stood there quietly and looked up at the farmhouse. The girls picked wild flowers growing along the roadway. Barbara watched the girls to make sure they didn't wander. Neil ran into the old horse barn to take one more look at the old sleigh.

"I'm so glad you invited me to come with you," Barbara said as she looked up at the house. "I know I will always have fond memories of this place."

"Maybe next time, Bill can come up and see the place. He would love it." I said.

"Sure, that would be nice," she agreed.

"I wish that we could have kept the place up better," I said, solemnly, noting the window panes broken and the paint pealing. "I know our lives are different now. Certain things come to an end and other things begin."

"Come on kids, let's get into the car, it's time to go," Barbara said calling for her girls as she opened the car door. Phyllis and Neil appeared from where they had been and tumbled into the car. But Margret and I continued to stand there a few minutes, not saying a word.

"We've done a lot of work on this place, had some good times and met some wonderful friends around here," I finally said with a soft voice to Margret. "But, it's time to go... time to go... home."

With tears in her eyes she said, "Good-bye Windhill Farms, we'll miss you."

"We'll be back," I said as I put my arms around her waist and guided her back to the car.

I got into the car and started the engine. I took one more look at the house before slowly driving off.

"We'll be back."

Phyllis Ellis was born and raised in Rye, New York. Like her father, she became an artist and made her living as a graphic designer and worked in NYC for ten years. Later she and her husband moved  to Georgia where she continued her graphic business in the Atlanta area. They moved to Flowery Branch, Georgia where they bought a farm and raised horses. When the farm was surrounded by subdivisions they decided to move to Dahlonega, Georgia. After her husband had died, she found her passion in painting, writing, and driving all through the United States and Canada.

40725101R00101

Made in the USA
Middletown, DE
21 February 2017